FILM MAKERS

15
GROUNDBREAKING
WOMEN DIRECTORS

**LYN MILLER-LACHMANN AND
TANISIA "TEE" MOORE**

CHICAGO REVIEW PRESS

Copyright © 2022 by Lyn Miller-Lachmann and Tanisia Moore

All rights reserved

First hardcover edition published in 2022

First paperback edition published in 2024

Published by Chicago Review Press Incorporated

814 North Franklin Street

Chicago, Illinois 60610

ISBN 979-8-89068-005-1

The Library of Congress has cataloged the hardcover edition under the following Control Number: 2022934946

Cover, illustrations, and interior design: Sadie Teper

Printed in the United States of America

For my grandmother, whose artistic dreams
showed me I could live my own.
—Lyn

For my forever muses, Syd, Savvy, and Jay . . .
Mommy loves you all. Forever and always.
—Tee

Contents

Introduction

In his well-known song, James Brown acknowledges that the world wouldn't be quite the same without a woman. Simply put, there's something powerful a woman brings to the table. In the past four decades, today's women filmmakers have dared to create stories that their male counterparts deemed too risky, too intimate, or too big. When the COVID-19 pandemic closed down schools, businesses, and communities, these women directors didn't stop working. They kept their crews and actors safe—in some cases going to extraordinary lengths to do so—while producing films that entertained and enlightened the masses of people trapped in their homes.

Yet oftentimes women are faced with strong opposition and barriers that attempt to keep them boxed into specific roles: the assistant working behind the scenes, receiving little or no credit; the "arm candy" valued for appearance rather than creativity, intelligence, or drive; the writer or director pushed to explore domestic topics when her dream is to make films about social upheaval, revolution, and war. But as this book will show, living outside this box is way more fun.

When Jane Campion, Agnieszka Holland, and Kathryn Bigelow began making films in the 1970s and '80s, women directors were a rarity. In 2010 Kathryn became the first woman in the decades-long history of the Academy Awards to receive the Oscar for Best Director, winning for *The Hurt Locker*. Sixteen years earlier, Jane was only the second woman *nominated* for that award, and her film, *The Piano*, did not win. And Chloé Zhao's independent film *Nomadland*, released in 2020, won Best Picture and Best Director at the 2021 Oscars and Golden Globes, making her the first woman of color to garner these prestigious prizes.

According to a report conducted by San Diego State University's Center for the Study of Women in Television and Film, "women comprised 21% of all directors, writers, producers, executive producers, editors, and cinematographers working on the top 100 grossing films in 2020" in the United States. However, the film industry has a long way to go in giving women—particularly women of color—an equal shot at the director's chair and other important positions behind the scenes. Hollywood has made great strides in showing diversity on set, casting more BIPOC (Black, Indigenous, and People of Color) actors, and while that is to be celebrated, the film industry still lacks diversity when it comes to directors, writers, and studio executives. Twenty-one percent is far from the fifty-one percent of women that represents the US population.

So how does one challenge this? By pushing back against the status quo in order to demand change. Ava DuVernay created "a personnel database for Hollywood's below-the-line crew members . . . 'designed to amplify women, people of color, and other underrepresented film and television professionals.'" One-on-one mentorship has served as another avenue for increasing the presence of women directors, particularly for women who are locked out of film programs due to a lack of money or who receive less attention in those programs because of their gender. Greta Gerwig credits a number of women directors who mentored her after she was rejected from multiple MFA programs and had to enter the industry through acting, rather than writing and directing as she had desired; she, in turn, is mentoring the young women who act in her films. Shonda Rhimes's shows inspired or directly launched the careers of other Black women filmmakers, such as Gina Prince-Bythewood and Issa Rae.

Each of the women profiled in the following chapters has faced some form of adversity in her career. The rejections these women faced created within them a commitment to keep pushing forward and to not allow a *no* to extinguish their passions.

Some of the women have escaped persecution from governments who were uncomfortable with their storytelling and wanted to silence them. For years, under the Communist regime in Poland, Agnieszka Holland was not credited for the work she did behind the scenes as a cinematographer and assistant director, because her father and she had run afoul of the authorities. She had to flee Poland in 1981 and start over in a new home, speaking a new language, in order to come into her own as a director. Two generations later, Chloé Zhao's parents sent her from China out of fear that her defiance of ancient traditions and modern rules would get her, and them, in trouble. Her work continues to face censorship in the country of her birth. These brave women filmmakers knew that their stories had to be shared so the next generation of young women would know that their voices matter and deserve to be heard.

Black women have especially played a major role in raising visibility and creating opportunities for themselves and other women of color, and the biographies in this volume reflect that role. Pioneering director Ava DuVernay explored the United States' struggles for racial justice in the documentary *13th* and docudramas *Selma* and *When They See Us*. Showrunners such as Shonda Rhimes have offered an entry point for younger women in the industry as they demonstrate to a white-dominated industry that Black stories sell. Dee Rees came out as gay while in film school in her late 20s, and she now confronts in her films the challenges of being both Black and LGBTQI+. Issa Rae has struggled with her identity as a Black woman who grew up in both US and Senegalese cultures.

This sense of living between two cultures informs the work of other filmmakers of color who bring forth fresh perspectives and universal truths. Lulu Wang was born in China but immigrated to the US at the age of six; her film *The Farewell* explores how these two cultures clash when a family is faced with a serious health crisis. Petra Costa moved to New York City from

Brazil against her mother's wishes after her older sister perished on the same journey 13 years earlier; her documentary *Elena* is a poetic tribute to her sister as well as plea to end the silence about suicide.

The careers of the 15 women filmmakers featured in this volume highlight a final theme that we explore: the range of their work, from documentaries and independent films to Hollywood blockbusters and popular TV shows. While some of the directors have made the switch from the art house to the megaplex—for instance, Chloé Zhao followed up *Nomadland* with *Eternals*, set in the Marvel universe—others go back and forth between film and TV work and between indie films and big-budget productions. Several of the directors have achieved critical and commercial success with adaptations of classic children's books, such as *The Secret Garden* (Agnieszka Holland), *Little Women* (Greta Gerwig), and *A Wrinkle in Time* (Ava DuVernay). In each case, the director put her spin on the book, as Ava cast the characters of Meg and her family with mostly Black actors, and Greta's *Little Women* has a strong feminist sensibility.

Our guiding principle in selecting these 15 filmmakers can be described by Shonda Rhimes herself: F.O.D.—"First. Only. Different." These phenomenal women have redefined the film and television industry, winning awards historically given to a male counterpart, being the only woman in a writers' room, or portraying stories no one else could tell. While their resumes are impressive, it is how they live their lives that has made a greater impact in their communities. By mentoring other women, standing up to those who seek to ignore or silence them, and telling their stories with passion and integrity, these women serve as role models and inspiration for future generations. We hope they will inspire you to use the tools of film to tell your story!

Part I
The Pioneer Generation

Jane Campion:
Passionate Film Trailblazer

Jane Campion was born into a family devoted to the arts. Her mother, Edith, was a writer and actor, and her father, Richard, directed theater and opera in Wellington, the capital and second largest city in New Zealand. When Jane arrived on April 30, 1954, she was the younger of two daughters; a brother would join them seven years later.

Because Edith inherited a large fortune from her grandfather, a shoe manufacturer, she and her family, including Jane and her older sister, Anna, could pursue their artistic dreams without worrying about money—to a point. In 1953 Richard and Edith founded a theater company, the New Zealand Players, which Edith supported financially.

This idyllic plan of raising three children amid theater, music, and literature in their remote corner of the world was soon shattered. The New Zealand Players hemorrhaged money and closed down in 1960. Accusations of improper behavior toward women dogged Richard at the theater and afterward, when he remained a part of the arts community as a teacher at Wellington College. Following the collapse of their joint enterprise, Edith wrote novel after novel loosely based on her unfaithful husband, troubled family life, and bouts of depression.

This unconventional and dysfunctional upbringing had a major impact on Jane as she grew up. She saw how her father's actions and behaviors had marginalized and isolated her mother. In 1992 as her acclaimed film *The Piano* was about to be released, she told Katherine Dieckmann of *Interview* magazine that as a child, she had not expected to have a creative career; rather, she "just thought, in the most unconscious fashion, that women don't have those sorts of careers, and if you're a talented woman you support a talented man."

In her teenage years Jane discovered the novels of the Brontë sisters. She became obsessed with these three women writers, especially Emily, the author of *Wuthering Heights*. She told the *Guardian* in 2018, "I always loved Emily Brontë's imagination. I feel like she saved my life, in the sense of giving me powerful female stories. To have that model for how a woman and an artist could be was very involving to me." Decades later *Wuthering Heights*, a gothic tale of passion set in a remote farmhouse in

Yorkshire, England, at the turn of the 19th century, would have a profound influence on Jane's breakout film, *The Piano*.

Despite her family's background and her own interest in both painting and literature, Jane initially rejected a creative career, instead majoring in anthropology at Victoria University of Wellington. At the same time, she wanted to see the world beyond her island nation of three million people and explore the possibilities of self-expression open to a young woman of nearly unlimited means and little direction for her life. She traveled to London, where she took classes in painting at the Chelsea School of Art and received a graduate degree in visual arts at the University of Sydney in Australia in 1981.

Even before finishing her degree program, she came to realize that her talents didn't lie in painting and that the medium was too limiting for the stories she wanted to tell. She signed up for more education, this time at the Australian Film, Television, and Radio School, graduating in 1984.

Jane began to make short films while studying painting in Australia. As a film school student and afterward, she wrote and directed many short films. *Peel*—a metaphor-filled journey of a father, daughter, and son—won the Short Film Palme d'Or at the 1986 Cannes Film Festival. Jane was the first woman director to receive this honor.

Jane has compared short films to short stories and called on critics and audiences to give more attention to this category. She has noted that since the 1980s, more women are making short films, in part to hone their skills (which nearly all young filmmakers do) and in part because it's harder for women to get funding for bigger projects.

Jane's first full-length feature was the dark comedy *Sweetie*, about a young Australian woman, Kay, whose relationships with her parents and her boyfriend are turned upside down when her troubled younger sister, Dawn (known as Sweetie), returns home to get her life back on track. Instead of getting control over her life, Sweetie wrecks everyone else's with her unbridled behavior. As with *Peel*, Jane uses metaphor—in this case a dying tree—to reveal her characters and foreshadow the ending.

Vincent Canby of the *New York Times* called *Sweetie* "a spectacular feature-film debut," saying, "It demands to be taken on its own spare terms without regard to the sentimental conventions of other movies." However, some of Jane's former champions at the Cannes Film Festival were not so impressed. Jane told Myra Forsberg of the *New York Times*, "I found the whole Cannes thing particularly upsetting because there were people who said, 'I'm absolutely shocked and disgusted by your film.' . . . There was this one guy—an Australian—who said, 'You have really shamed me.'"

Undaunted by the criticism, Jane continued to push the limits of filmmaking categories and taboos. In her next feature film, *An Angel at My Table*, which was originally conceived as a three-part TV series and runs more than two and a half hours, she explored the life of renowned New Zealand author Janet Frame. This 1990 release isn't a polite documentary about an author whose books are regularly taught in advanced high school literature classes in the English-speaking world but rather a portrayal of the childhood poverty, isolation, misdiagnosed mental illness, and institutionalization that defined Frame's life and work.

In her adaptation of Frame's three-volume autobiography, Jane cast unglamorous red-haired actors to portray the author at various stages of her life. The protagonist's awkward presence is juxtaposed with the stunning landscape of rural New Zealand and the places in Europe where Frame lived after her release from the mental hospital. The scenes inside the hospital are harrowing. The film shows Frame receiving electroshock therapy and scheduled for a lobotomy—a crude operation that would have destroyed her creative mind and kept her dependent for the rest of her life—when one of her books won a major award and the procedure was cancelled.

An Angel at My Table won numerous international awards, and critics lauded the performances of child actor Alexia Keogh. Roger Ebert justified the film's long run time, calling it "strangely engrossing from beginning to end."

After working with one child actor, Jane next directed the film that would launch the career of 11-year-old Anna Paquin and make history for both Anna and Jane. Released in 1993, *The Piano* is a historical drama set in New Zealand in 1850, as

British settlers were beginning to encroach on lands inhabited by the Maori people. Jane's original screenplay about a mute woman who escapes from her cruel and controlling husband into the arms of one of her husband's employees draws inspiration from the 19th-century romantic fiction of Mary Shelley, Jane Austen, and the Brontë sisters. As in *An Angel at My Table*, the remote New Zealand landscape is a powerful presence, creating a somber, foreboding mood for the story. Like *Sweetie*, metaphors convey the story's meaning. While Ada, Jane's protagonist, cannot speak, she communicates through music and finds emotional fulfillment in defiance of her husband and the violent patriarchal society that he embodies. Music is how this woman finds her voice.

Anna Paquin

Anna was born on July 24, 1982, in Winnipeg, Manitoba. Her mother came to Canada from Wellington, New Zealand, and her father is Canadian. When she was four, her family moved to New Zealand, where in 1991 she and her sister saw a newspaper ad to audition for Jane's film. Both tried out, as did some five thousand other children in New Zealand, but Anna won the role.

After this success, Anna accepted other acting opportunities as a teenager, among them roles in *Jane Eyre*, *Fly Away Home*, *A Walk on the Moon*, *Amistad*, and *Almost*

Famous. Her work in *Fly Away Home*, the 1996 film from Canada about a widowed father and his daughter who guide 16 abandoned goslings to their winter home, netted several award nominations.

Looking back on her debut performance, Anna considers it a lucky accident that Jane took her on for the role of protagonist Ada's 10-year-old daughter and inspired her to make her own impact in the film industry. As she told the *Hollywood Reporter* in 2019, *The Piano* "was this massive female filmmaker fest. My formative experience was, 'Of course women do those jobs.'"

Critics hailed *The Piano* as the best film of 1993. Roger Ebert called it "as peculiar and haunting as any film I've seen." Vincent Canby wrote, "The film looks deceptively small, but in character it's big and strong and complex. Here's a severely beautiful, mysterious movie that, as if by magic, liberates the romantic imagination." While noting the R-rated film is appropriate only for mature teens and adults, Common Sense Media—an organization that advocates for family-friendly media and evaluates for age-appropriateness—gave *The Piano* five out of five stars in recognition of its high literary and cinematic quality.

The Piano broke ground during awards season. Jane became the first woman director to win the Palme d'Or, the highest award at the Cannes Film Festival. She was the second woman to receive an Academy Award nomination for Best Director and won an Oscar for Best Original Screenplay. Anna Paquin received Best Supporting Actress, making her the second-youngest actor to win an Oscar.

Lina Wertmüller and *Seven Beauties*

Her name may sound German, but Lina Wertmüller was born in Rome, Italy, in 1928. She was descended from Swiss nobility on her father's side, and her parents were devout Catholics, an upbringing against which she rebelled. Her love of comic books in the 1930s and 1940s led her first into puppetry and then into filmmaking, when in the early 1960s she met Federico Fellini, one of the greatest directors of all time.

At first Lina directed films under a man's pseudonym to avoid prejudice against women in the industry. She came into her own in the 1970s, releasing seven feature films under her own name that gained international acclaim. Most of these were dark comedies, including *Seven Beauties*, which made her the first woman to receive an Academy Award nomination for Best Director.

Jane's triumph at the Cannes Film Festival, however, coincided with a terrible personal tragedy. In 1992 she married one of her assistant directors, Colin Englert, and shortly afterward became pregnant with their first child. During the festival, she experienced complications and rushed back to Australia, where she gave birth to a boy who lived only eleven days. "I really didn't enjoy any of the success. It almost felt like 'at the cost of,'" she later told Kate Muir of the *Guardian*.

After months of grieving her son's death and giving birth to her daughter, Alice, a year later, Jane returned to making films. Her next release, in 1996, was an adaptation of Henry James's 19th-century classic *The Portrait of a Lady*. She followed that with *Holy Smoke!*, a comedy about a woman who has joined a New Age cult and the male counselor who is hired to deprogram her and falls in love with her. Jane wrote the screenplay with her older sister, Anna, who followed her into the film industry.

In 2003 Jane released *In the Cut*, a thriller based on a novel by American author Susanna Moore. It is the most commercial of her films and the one that almost ended her career. After the mixed reviews and poor box-office showing of *Holy Smoke!*, *In the Cut* garnered mostly negative reviews and mediocre ticket sales.

At that point, Jane decided to take a lengthy break. She and Colin had divorced in 2001, and Alice was struggling. In an interview for the *Guardian*, she said,

I was going to take a break anyway . . . but I found it really easy, because when you have a failure, nobody rings you up or wants you to do anything. I just wanted to be with my kid a bit more and spent four years being more of a mother. I actually had to convince her that, "I am your mother."

Jane homeschooled Alice for four years. When Alice was 13, she told Jane she wanted to become an actor. Since then, Jane has helped develop her young daughter's career along with her own.

Alice Englert: A New Generation of Artists

On June 15, 1994, one year after her son Jasper's death, Jane gave birth to Alice, who spent much of her early years with nannies while her mother wrote and directed three films. Alice left high school early to become an actor, learning at the side of the mother who had home-schooled her for four years. At the age of 12, she acted in Jane's short film *The Water Diary*, which portrays a child survivor of a drought. Her first performance in a feature film was the 2012 friendship story *Ginger and Rosa*, set in London in the 1960s and directed by British filmmaker Sally Potter.

Alice acted in the 2013 film adaptation of the best-selling young adult novel *Beautiful Creatures* and composed one of the songs for the film's soundtrack. She played major roles in five TV series in the 2010s, including Jane's acclaimed *Top of the Lake: China Girl*. Alice wrote and directed two short films, the 2015 drama *The Boyfriend Game* and the 2017 story of sibling relationships and rivalries *Family Happiness*. She maintains a close relationship with her mother, telling *thisNZlife*, "I think she's fantastic, she's one of the best filmmakers in the world, and so it's been easy, and I just do what she wants—or at least try to do what she wants."

Jane returned to biographical films of literary figures in 2009 with *Bright Star*. It portrays the romantic relationship between early-19th-century poet John Keats, dying of tuberculosis in his early 20s, and his muse, Fanny Brawne.

After three decades of making feature films and shorts, Jane next turned to television in search of "creative freedom." She told the *Guardian*'s Simon Hattenstone, "Cinema in Australia and New Zealand has become much more mainstream. It's broad entertainment. . . . But in television, there is no concern about politeness or pleasing the audience."

Codirected and coauthored by Jane, *Top of the Lake* was her first TV series. Set in New Zealand, *Top of the Lake* is a mystery featuring Elisabeth Moss as Robin Griffin, a detective working on cases of violence against women; it spawned a companion series four years later. In the first series, which aired in 2013, Robin investigates the disappearance of a 12-year-old girl. The second series, *Top of the Lake: China Girl*, which aired in 2017, takes place in Sydney, Australia, where Robin investigates the death of a young Asian surrogate mother on Bondi Beach. In this second season, Alice Englert played the role of Robin's troubled 17-year-old daughter, with whom she seeks to rekindle a relationship over the course of the series.

In *Top of the Lake*, as in *The Piano* and her other acclaimed films, Jane has explored family dynamics and women's ability to carve out a space for action against the forces of patriarchy. From the real writer Janet Frame, whose published stories saved her from destruction, to the mute fictional character Ada McGrath, who used her music to resist a brutal colonizer husband, Jane's characters refuse to be silenced.

In 2021 Jane's career took an unexpected turn. Although having previously said she would never make another feature film, she adapted the 1967 western novel *The Power of the Dog* into a story of toxic masculinity and its destructive effects— one in which women play a secondary role but a gay teenage boy finds his voice. Like *The Piano* and her biographical films, *The Power of the Dog* is set in the past, in Montana in 1925. One powerful man, the wealthy rancher Phil Burbank, terrorizes everyone around him by exploiting their emotional vulnerabilities while carefully guarding his own. In an interview for the

Hollywood Reporter, Jane talked about Phil's family wealth and how that enables him to abuse others without consequences: "I think power is always the real issue. . . . And money is often power."

Connecting her protagonist's power to the role of money and drawing on her past success in the film industry, Jane added that power "comes through with women too, when they have power and how they choose to use it." Having seen what happened to her mother at the hands of an unsupportive husband, Jane has used her considerable talents to make an enduring impact on the global film industry. After becoming a mother and gaining her own base of power within the industry, she continues to inspire and assist young women who want to act or work behind the camera. With the support of Netflix, she is closing the circle on her family history by starting a film school in New Zealand, in this way helping the next generation of women filmmakers to make their mark.

Agnieszka Holland: The Cinema of Moral Anxiety

Several years after Hurricane Katrina devastated the city of New Orleans, the award-winning TV showrunner David Simon conceived a series that would portray the diverse people of the city trying to rebuild their lives and their community. The series, *Treme*, centered around the working-class community of Tremé, a place of jazz clubs and of Black history spanning nearly five centuries. Although the neighborhood didn't suffer as much as others from the 2005 hurricane, most of the buildings sustained both water and wind damage.

The pilot can make or break a TV series. Networks order more episodes after a successful pilot, but if it fails to draw or satisfy an audience, no one will see the show again. David already had a hit series in *The Wire*, set among drug gangs, corrupt politicians, and reformers in Baltimore, Maryland. When he announced his plans for *Treme*, fans and critics wondered who would direct the all-important pilot.

His choice, the 60-year-old Polish director Agnieszka Holland, shocked many. Not only was she not from New Orleans and not Black, she wasn't even from the United States. She had directed several episodes of *The Wire*, though, and she'd impressed David with her visual sense and her staging of fights and shootouts. In meeting the challenge of depicting the hurricane-battered city, she said she was "thinking about Poland just after World War II," adding, "there are lots of things that can be taken from there."

Born on November 28, 1948, in a Warsaw under Communist control and just beginning to rebuild from the war, Agnieszka is the daughter of two prominent journalists who had fought against the Nazis. Her father, Henryk Holland, was Jewish, and his parents perished in the Holocaust. Both of Agnieszka's parents rose through the Communist Party ranks, but in 1961, Henryk was arrested, accused of leaking classified information to Western journalists in the midst of the Cold War, which divided Europe, with Eastern Europe dominated by the Soviet Union. Henryk died under suspicious circumstances while in police custody when Agnieszka, his older of two daughters, was 13.

Because of her father's Jewish roots and the circumstances of his death, Agnieszka was urged to use her mother's surname or, later on, that of her husband, the Slovak filmmaker Laco

Adamik. She refused. Years later she told the *New York Times*, "Certainly the mystery of my father's death has played a big role in my art. . . . It gave me a kind of rebellion."

After her father's death, Agnieszka turned to writing and dreamed of making films. Because of her background, the film schools in Poland would not accept her, so she applied to the Film and TV School of the Academy of Performing Arts, known as FAMU, in Prague, Czechoslovakia (now the Czech Republic), where some of the most prominent filmmakers in Eastern Europe, including Miloš Forman and Věra Chytilová, had studied.

Věra Chytilová: Director of Czechoslovak New Wave Cinema

Four years before Agnieszka began her studies at FAMU, another woman director, Věra Chytilová, received her degree from the prestigious film school. That another woman could study film and then direct her own served as an inspiration for Agnieszka as she prepared to enter a world dominated by men. Born in 1929 in Ostrava, an industrial city in Czechoslovakia, Věra eventually moved to Prague, where she worked as a model among other odd jobs and found low-level work at the state-owned film studios. Refusing to give up her dreams despite her bosses' lack of support, she applied to FAMU and made two short films there that introduced her to Czech audiences.

Věra's first feature film, *Something Different*, was released in 1963 and tells the story of two women, a frustrated housewife and an Olympic athlete, who meet in one of the opening scenes before their paths diverge. Her 1966 film, *Daisies*, depicts two rebellious teenage girls whose pranks escalate into destructive and dangerous acts. The government banned *Daisies* after its showing at film festivals due to its negative images of the country's youth.

Věra became one of the principal directors of the Czechoslovak New Wave of the 1960s. Rather than pretend everyone under the country's Communist regime was happy and prosperous, these directors showed the way people actually lived, and they poked fun at government officials and arbitrary rules. After the 1968 Soviet invasion, many Czech directors fled the country. Věra decided to stay even though her films were banned. She raised her children and directed TV commercials using her husband's surname. She was allowed to make films again in the late 1970s after an international campaign on her behalf and a personal appeal to the country's leader, which included submitting to government censorship.

After the fall of Communism in Eastern Europe in 1989,

Věra continued to make irreverent films and taught film-making at FAMU. She died in 2014 at the age of 85.

Until August 21, 1968, the students at FAMU and else-where in Czechoslovakia enjoyed freedoms unavailable to young people elsewhere in Eastern Europe. It was the time of the Prague Spring, when the country's Communist Party leaders implemented reforms to encourage discussion and innovation. The Soviet Union, which controlled the governments of its satellite nations, feared that Czechoslovakia would leave its bloc and join the West as a result. With the assistance of four other nations, including Poland, the Soviets invaded and occupied Czechoslovakia, removing the reform government and imposing harsh censorship.

While protesting the invasion, Agnieszka was arrested and imprisoned for six weeks. There, she found herself passing messages between two other prisoners who were lovers, in a way eavesdropping on their relationship. In the future, many of her films would place the audience in the position of eavesdropping on illicit relationships.

After graduating from FAMU in 1971, Agnieszka returned to Poland with Laco, and their daughter, Katerzyna "Kasia" Adamik, was born a year later. The famous Polish director Andrzej Wajda mentored Agnieszka, and she absorbed his fascination with the psychology of the protagonist. By focusing on complex main characters and the difficult moral choices they are forced to make, Agnieszka, like her mentor, was able to question Communist beliefs and the realities of life in Poland. Before long, she became one of the principal directors of the cinema of moral anxiety, defined as "a genre deeply entrenched in the reality of 1970s Poland (characterised by showing human struggles to maintain dignity under the most trying circumstances)." One of her first feature films, *Provincial Actors* (1979), explores the power struggle between an aging actor and a woman theater director, further complicated by the actor's wife, who also wants a part in the play. It's a story of interpersonal and professional intrigue, but one that subtly shows the individual's loss of agency under a bureaucratic Communist regime.

Agnieszka directed three TV specials and three feature films in Poland before 1981, when outside events changed the course of her life again. In August 1980 a national strike caused the government to grant more freedom to the Polish people in exchange for them returning to work. This period of liberalization reminded Agnieszka of the rights to speak out, create, and travel that she had enjoyed when she was studying at FAMU during the Prague Spring. But while she was in Western Europe promoting her films in 1981, the government invited Soviet forces back into the country, cracked down on all dissent, and arrested the leaders of the previous year's strike.

Unwilling to return to a harsh dictatorship, Agnieszka settled in France, where she was granted asylum. Agnieszka didn't speak the language and had to leave her daughter behind. It was one of the hardest periods of her life, as she told Roger Cohen of the *New York Times*:

> It was eight months . . . of total isolation, before I saw [Kasia]. The poor girl was 9, she could not understand. . . . When my daughter arrived in France, she would not speak to me for weeks. Later, Kasia told me she had been sure that I was dead.

In the next few years, Agnieszka learned both French and English and began to travel throughout the West—a new way of life for someone raised amid the restrictions of Soviet-controlled Eastern Europe. She also began to explore in her films the lives of people like her—trapped by forces in history, fighting to take back some control over their lives, and making questionable moral choices in the process.

The Holocaust proved fertile ground for this filmmaker of Jewish heritage. Her first film after fleeing Poland, *Angry Harvest* (1985), portrays a Jewish family that jumps from a train on its way to a concentration camp. The members of the family hide in separate locations, the mother finding refuge with a Catholic farmer. She ends up having an affair with the farmer, with tragic results. The film, produced in what was then West Germany, was nominated for an Academy Award for Best Foreign Language Film.

Agnieszka followed this film with the acclaimed 1990 release *Europa Europa*, which was based on the true story of Solomon Perel, a Jewish teenager who survived the Holocaust by pretending to be a Nazi. Agnieszka's adaptation (with German screenwriter Paul Hengge) of Perel's autobiography received a nomination for Best Adapted Screenplay at the 1992 Academy Awards and won that year's Golden Globe for Best Foreign Language Film.

The third film in Agnieszka's Holocaust trilogy, *In Darkness*, came out two decades later, in 2011. By this time, Communist regimes had collapsed throughout eastern Europe, and she could work with Polish actors to make the film. At first she resisted yet another treatment of that subject, telling the *New York Times* reporter Larry Rohter, "It was very costly, painful to spend two years of your life or more in this world, which certainly changes something in your body and soul." But a wealthy Canadian writer-producer approached her with his screen adaptation of the true story of a small-time Polish criminal who, along with robbing a group of Jews, hid them in the sewers of Lwów, Poland (now Lviv, Ukraine), until the Soviet army could liberate them. The idea of a "terrible" person engaging in acts of heroism—and the difficult personalities of many of the people he rescued—as well as the artistic challenge of shooting the film in a sewer, appealed to Agnieszka:

> I found it crucial for the actors to be in the real darkness. . . . Another thing I wanted to avoid was to make those sewers too spectacular. . . . It's very difficult to work there. You feel really bad after one hour. It was difficult to imagine how they can accommodate themselves for such a long time to these circumstances.

In Darkness received an Academy Award nomination—this time nominated by Poland—for Best Foreign Language Film. Although Agnieszka did not win the prize, the film received multiple nominations at European film festivals and the grand prize in festivals in Poland, Spain, Romania, and the UK.

Following in Agnieszka's Footsteps: Jasmila Žbanić

Less than four decades after the world learned of the Holocaust and pledged "never again," the Muslim communities of the former Yugoslavia—a Communist country that had broken apart after the fall of the Soviet empire—endured another genocide, this time at the hands of Serb leaders and their militias. Born in in 1974 in Sarajevo, Bosnia and Herzegovina—then part of Yugoslavia—

Jasmila Žbanić left for the United States in the early 1990s, shortly after Communist rule ended in her country, when she could travel freely. For several years she worked with Vermont's popular Bread and Puppet Theater. Those years marked the height of Serb attacks on her home and her Muslim people.

When Jasmila returned to Sarajevo in the late 1990s, she sought to make films about the war and its aftermath, telling the stories of friends and neighbors who survived the violence that she'd avoided while living abroad. Her most famous film, *Quo Vadis, Aida?*, came out in 2020 and was nominated for the Academy Award for Best International Feature Film. This powerful drama focuses on a Bosnian Muslim teacher and United Nations translator from Srebrenica who tries to smuggle her husband and two sons to safety with the UN delegation after besieged UN commanders hand thousands of Bosnian Muslim refugees over to Serb paramilitary forces.

Agnieszka's desire to present unexpected heroes, intricate moral dilemmas, and complex, flawed, and often unlikeable protagonists—what distinguished her Holocaust films from those of other directors—made her a good match for adaptations of great literary works. She directed the 1993 version of Frances Hodgson Burnett's novel *The Secret Garden*. Critics praised her representation of the spoiled, demanding orphan Mary Lennox, who finds friendship and purpose in the garden of her uncle's crumbling estate. Common Sense Media called it "a fine adaptation of the beloved children's book," and two decades after its release, it continues to find an audience.

In 2017 Agnieszka released *Spoor*, her adaptation of Nobel Prize–winning Polish author Olga Tokarczuk's novel *Drive Your Plough over the Bones of the Dead*. Agnieszka and Olga coauthored the screenplay about a 60-year-old woman, a retired engineer and lover of animals, who moves to a Polish mountain village to teach English, only to discover the men there enjoy hunting for sport. When her two dogs disappear and villagers die in mysterious circumstances, this strange, difficult, almost universally disrespected protagonist teams up with more local misfits—a reclusive widower, a young neurodivergent IT expert, a shopgirl trying to get custody of her younger brother, and a visiting Czech entomologist—to find the perpetrators. Having followed her mother into the film industry, Kasia codirected *Spoor* with Agnieszka and worked with the animals that played a major role in the movie.

Though generally well received, *Spoor* created a stir on the festival circuit. The unreliable narrator confused and angered some critics, and others, especially in Poland, condemned it as "a deeply anti-Christian film that promoted eco-terrorism," which prompted Agnieszka to reply, "We read that with some satisfaction and we are thinking of putting it on the promotional posters, because it will encourage people who might otherwise not have bothered to come and see it."

Although Agnieszka's 2019 film, *Mr. Jones*, did not adapt a major work of literature, it draws from George Orwell's *Animal Farm* in its depiction of the Holodomor, also known as the Terror-Famine, that killed millions of Ukrainians in the 1930s. The film begins with pigs in a sty and the novel's famous line: "All animals are equal, but some animals are more equal than others." The Mr. Jones of the film is not the farm's owner, driven away by a four-legged revolution, but the real-life Welsh journalist Gareth Jones, who peers behind the artificial prosperity of Moscow under Stalin's Communist dictatorship. He discovers that Ukrainian peasants are left to starve as their grain is confiscated by the government to feed the ruling party and to create an illusion for the West that Communism brings prosperity. Mr. Jones does not run away, but when he reports the truth, few mainstream journalists believe him. Agnieszka worked from a script by Ukrainian American journalist Andrea Chalupa, who has warned of the dangers of a new wave of authoritarianism around the world.

In the past two decades, Agnieszka has turned increasingly to TV, often directing multiple projects at the same time in Europe and the US. She observes in a BBC interview that "television became much more innovative on the level of storytelling." She continued, "For the audiovisual generation, television was more courageous, new and exciting," Agnieszka became one of the innovators of this medium. In addition to her work on *The Wire, Treme, Cold Case, The Killing,* and *House of Cards,* she directed crime dramas in Poland and HBO Europe's first major TV miniseries, *Burning Bush.*

Broadcast in 2013 and considered by critics to be one of her finest works, the three-part, four-hour miniseries *Burning Bush* portrays what happened after university student Jan Palach set himself on fire in Prague in 1969 to protest the Soviet invasion the previous year—the same invasion that Agnieszka had lived through as a student at FAMU and had gone to prison for opposing. Her scriptwriter, the Czech film historian Štěpán Hulík, was only 29 years old, which gave her the opportunity to work with a young writer who shared her desire to address their respective countries' painful pasts. Like the characters in Agnieszka's movies, the ensemble cast of *Burning Bush* consists of complex individuals faced with terrible personal and moral choices because of the brutal dictatorship in which they lived. Among them are a university official who betrays his faculty and students in order to protect his rebellious teenage daughter and a courageous lawyer whose actions cause her husband to lose his job.

With a career spanning 50 years and dozens of feature films, shorts, TV episodes, and miniseries, Agnieszka is one of the most prolific and versatile directors in the industry. She is no stranger to controversy, but even those who have criticized her work, denounced her for not presenting their black-and-white view of the world, or tried to censor her have to respect her. She has achieved stunning success in a field dominated by men. She has fought against brutal regimes that took away freedom in her birth country and the country where she received her education, and she has uncovered the untold stories of others who stood up against repression, violence, and genocide. She has shown that imperfect people can be heroes and seemingly good people can do terrible things—or else do nothing and let terrible things happen. In the pilot of *Treme*, one of the characters calls New Orleans during Hurricane Katrina a "man-made disaster." Agnieszka has chronicled the man-made disasters of the past century and the current one with insight, intelligence, and unforgettable images, characters, and stories.

Kathryn Bigelow:
Breaking Out in a Man's World

The red carpet rolls out for the Oscars. As the guests arrive at the theater for the ceremony, photographers' bulbs flash, and pictures of the celebrities and their outfits make their way onto social media. Months of media buzz over the nominations and the potential winners come down to one night, televised for millions of viewers in the United States and around the world.

The 82nd Academy Awards celebration on March 7, 2010, attracted special attention. It was only the fourth time a woman had been nominated for Best Director. Neither Lina Wertmüller for *Seven Beauties* nor Jane Campion for *The Piano* nor Sofia Coppola for *Lost in Translation* had carried home the golden Best Director Oscar statue. Now it was Kathryn Bigelow's turn. Her film, *The Hurt Locker*, had been nominated for nine awards, including Best Picture—the same number of nominations received by her ex-husband James Cameron's blockbuster science-fiction thriller *Avatar*. Cameron, sitting behind her at the ceremony, had already won the Golden Globe for Best Director for *Avatar*. It seemed that, once again, a man would walk away with the prize.

To the tune of her classic song "The Way We Were," singer, actor, and director Barbra Streisand strode onto the stage to announce the Best Director award. Noting that both a woman, Bigelow, and an African American director, Lee Daniels, were on the nominee list, Streisand described this award as an opportunity for the Academy to make history. She read the names and films of the five nominees. Then she opened the envelope and smiled. "Well, the time has come," she said and announced, "Kathryn Bigelow."

The Hurt Locker, the story of an American bomb-disposal team in Iraq and its leader's struggle to adjust to civilian life, would go on to win awards for Best Picture, Best Original Screenplay, Best Film Editing, Best Sound Editing, and Best Sound Mixing. It would catapult Kathryn into the top echelon of directors, following three decades of flops and modest successes, collaborations with her former husband, and efforts to break out of his shadow. It would also cement her reputation as a director of "big" films, made under the most challenging of circumstances and addressing violence, social upheaval, and war—topics traditionally seen as the realm of male storytellers.

James Cameron: Hitmaker

Kathryn was married to the Canadian-born director James Cameron for two years, from 1989 to 1991, and they continued to collaborate after their divorce. He cowrote and produced her 1995 sci-fi thriller *Strange Days*, set in a crime-ridden Los Angeles in the near future. The film reflected his sensibility more than hers. Before then, he was best known for *Aliens*, *The Terminator* and its sequel, and *The Abyss*, and he would go on to make the popular *Avatar* movie—all of them futuristic thrillers acclaimed for their nonstop action and innovative special effects. James's sole Academy Award for Best Director (and Best Picture), however, was not for his signature sci-fi films but for the blockbuster 1997 historical drama *Titanic*, a romance between a young society woman and a starving artist set amid the doomed maiden voyage of the luxury ship.

Kathryn Bigelow, the daughter of a factory manager and a school librarian, was born on November 27, 1951, in San Carlos, California, just south of San Francisco. After her family moved to southern California, she attended high school in suburban Orange County.

At first Kathryn wanted to study painting. She began her studies at the San Francisco Art Institute in 1970, then moved across the country to New York City after winning a prestigious scholarship to the Whitney Museum's Independent Study Program. There, she became friends with artists Richard Serra, Robert Rauschenberg, and Julian Schnabel and the musician Philip Glass.

In spite of the hardships of living in New York City in the 1970s—such as the high cost of living, which necessitated her to take up a side job fixing up distressed buildings—Kathryn looked forward to a promising career as a painter. All that changed when she saw Sam Peckinpah's classic film *The Wild Bunch*. This dark western set in the early 20th century shocked many viewers for its graphic violence, much of it conveyed in blood-soaked slow-motion sequences. As she stated in a *60 Minutes* interview with Lesley Stahl in 2010, these same techniques fascinated Kathryn, both for their artistry and for their ability to make viewers identify with the characters, "to feel what they feel."

Kathryn pursued a master of fine arts in film at Columbia University and received her degree in 1981. Her solo directorial debut, *Near Dark*, released in 1987, blended two genres—western and horror—reflecting the influence of *The Wild Bunch*. Though the reviews were mostly favorable and the movie attracted a cult following, initial ticket sales were poor. Her next two films, *Blue Steel* (1990) and *Point Break* (1991), were crime thrillers set in the places where she had lived most of her life—New York City for *Blue Steel* and among southern

California's surfer culture for *Point Break*. The latter film, which stars Keanu Reeves as an undercover FBI officer infiltrating a criminal gang of surfers, achieved more commercial success than each of her other films up to that point.

Following her sci-fi collaboration with James Cameron, *Strange Days*, and a 2000 mystery adapting Anita Shreve's novel *The Weight of Water* that released to negative reviews and, again, poor ticket sales, Kathryn turned her focus to the subjects that would define her work for the next two decades— real-life social conflicts and war. Even then, she didn't find immediate success.

Released in 2002, *K-19: The Widowmaker* recounts the story of a Soviet nuclear submarine faced with a meltdown deep below the surface of the North Atlantic Ocean in 1961, at the height of the Cold War. Bigelow worked with a team of people from the United Kingdom, Canada, and Germany to portray this tension-filled race against time and the enclosed space that could have become a tomb for 139 crew members or touched off World War III had the submarine exploded. While the film fictionalized events in ways that angered survivors of the disaster—including the depiction of a mutiny that never occurred—they and many critics praised Kathryn's re-creation of the setting and the crew's heroic response to the reactor's overheating and the spread of deadly radiation. With a budget of almost $100 million but earnings of about $65 million worldwide, *K-19* was considered a flop, one that would make it more difficult for her to raise the money for subsequent projects.

After a hiatus of six years when Kathryn couldn't raise the money for her own projects and had to work on other people's projects, such as directing one episode of the short-lived TV police thriller *Karen Sisco*, *The Hurt Locker* offered her another chance to make an impact. She got in touch with Mark Boal, a journalist who had tagged along with a roadside bomb disposal team in Iraq for two weeks in 2004 and written a feature about it for *Playboy* magazine in 2005. In an interview with Mark for the Associated Press in 2009, she explained her motivation:

> As a member of the general public, I felt this conflict was fairly abstract and perhaps under-reported. . . . When he [Mark] came back from Baghdad with all this information, these extraordinary stories about these men who arguably have the most dangerous job in the world—and yet it's a volunteer military, so they're there by choice—I thought it was a pretty extraordinary psychology and potentially rich for a character study.

The war itself was controversial, based on unproven assertions that the Iraqi dictator Saddam Hussein had weapons of mass destruction and assisted the planners of the September

11, 2001, terrorist attacks. Although US and coalition forces toppled Hussein in April 2003 after less than a month of combat, the invasion resistance turned to guerrilla warfare, with costly and tragic results on all sides. Mark's screenplay, which Kathryn brought to life in the film, shows those costs to the Iraqi population and the US troops.

In an interview for the *Guardian*, Kathryn talked about the political implications of *The Hurt Locker*. She said, "I'm drawn to provocative characters" and described war as a "great crucible." She added that, as was the case with *K-19*, "I avoid speeches in films but not politics" and observed that her characters are there "by virtue of politics." In her *60 Minutes* interview, Lesley Stahl summarizes Kathryn's position of seeing the film "both as antiwar and as a tribute to the soldiers who sign up to do this kind of work."

Kathryn filmed *The Hurt Locker* in Jordan near the border with Iraq in the summer of 2008. In this desert setting, temperatures rose above 110 degrees in daytime, and moviegoers can see the effects of the relentless heat on the characters. Kathryn filmed scenes with four different cameras, four different angles, so the actors didn't know where to focus their gaze. This adds to the film's realism, not least because the characters are in a place where they can be attacked from any side at any moment.

The praise for *The Hurt Locker* exceeded anything Kathryn had experienced before. A. O. Scott wrote in the *New York*

Times, "If 'The Hurt Locker' is not the best action movie of the summer, I'll blow up my car." Scott's car remained intact. Comparing *The Hurt Locker* to more overtly antiwar films, Peter Bradshaw of the *Guardian* wrote, "Bigelow says more about the agony and tragedy of war than all those earnest, well-meaning movies." Roger Ebert called *The Hurt Locker* "a great film, an intelligent film, a film shot clearly so that we know exactly who everybody is and where they are and what they're doing and why."

Kathryn's budget to make the film, $15 million, was far smaller than her budget for *K-19*, and the opening week box-office sales did not bode well for its success. Kathryn, however, remained "undaunted by any potential for it not to work out" due to the strength of the material and the hard work of Mark, her actors, her crew, and herself. Critical praise and major awards led to a solid profit over time, thus opening the door to bigger budgets and even more ambitious projects. Again calling on Mark's journalism and writing skills, Kathryn seized that opportunity to make one of the most controversial films in recent history.

Seen as a companion to *The Hurt Locker*, *Zero Dark Thirty* started out in 2010 as a story of the hunt for Osama bin Laden, the mastermind of the September 11 attacks. Mark had almost finished the screenplay on May 2, 2011, when a US Navy SEAL team attacked the compound in Abbottabad, Pakistan, where bin Laden was living and killed the al-Qaeda leader. Kathryn and Mark ditched their script and created a new one that focused on the events leading to bin Laden's elimination, as experienced through the eyes of the fictional CIA operative Maya, played by Jessica Chastain.

Brought to a clandestine prison in order to interrogate al-Qaeda prisoners, Maya overcomes her scruples against torture and uses waterboarding (a method that simulates drowning) and other brutal techniques to gain information, though she ultimately realizes that less violent interrogation techniques yield better results. Maya has to convince her colleagues and CIA higher-ups that she is "100 percent certain" that bin Laden is in the Abbottabad compound and that they should risk sending their elite forces to get him. The film begins with recordings of 9/11 victims' final conversations with their loved ones and ends with a 25-minute re-creation of the attack on bin Laden, filmed with a handheld camera and night-vision goggles to convey the chaos and peril. In between are graphic scenes of interrogations along with Maya and her colleagues' efforts to piece together the clues they receive from the prisoners and other sources while dodging new terrorist attacks in their undisclosed locations.

Most critics praised *Zero Dark Thirty*. Manohla Dargis of the *New York Times* called it "brilliantly directed . . . a cool, outwardly nonpartisan intelligence procedural." She added, "It is also a wrenchingly sad, soul-shaking story about revenge and its moral costs, which makes it the most important American fiction movie about Sept. 11."

Kathryn lost some critics, notably Peter Bradshaw of the *Guardian*, who praised her technical skill but wrote that the film "sticks solemnly and submissively to the CIA's official version of events," saying that "the waterboarding scenes are unwatchably horrible."

Nominated for five Academy Awards, including Best Actress, Best Original Screenplay, and Best Picture, *Zero Dark Thirty* only took one prize, for Best Sound Editing. It had more success at the box office. Produced with a budget of $40 million, the film took in $95 million in the United States and nearly $133 million worldwide.

Congress Weighs In

Zero Dark Thirty attracted attention from the US Congress as well, not all of it favorable. Representative Peter King, a New York Republican, questioned whether the film used classified information, accusing screenwriter Mark Boal of sneaking into a CIA briefing after bin Laden's death. Republican senator from Arizona and former presidential candidate John McCain—himself a survivor of torture when his plane was shot down during the Vietnam War—objected to any suggestion that it was a legitimate method of getting information from captives. In a

CNN interview, he said, "Torture does not work. It is hateful. It is harmful, incredibly harmful, to the United States of America, and to somehow make people believe it was responsible for the elimination of Osama bin Laden is in my view unacceptable."

Kathryn responded to concerns about her graphic depiction of torture in the film. Using the CIA's euphemism, "enhanced interrogation techniques," she claimed that critics "mischaracterized" the film when they said it emphasized the role of torture in obtaining key information about bin Laden's associates and location. She also defended the presence of these scenes in the film. "To have eliminated it [torture] would have meant we would have been whitewashing that story," she told Peter Travers in a 2013 interview for ABC News. In a statement published in the *Los Angeles Times*, she went further:

As a lifelong pacifist, I support all protests against the use of torture, and, quite simply, inhumane treatment of any kind.

But I do wonder if some of the sentiments alternately expressed about the film might be more appropriately directed at those who instituted and ordered these U.S. policies, as opposed to a motion picture that brings the story to the screen.

Those of us who work in the arts know that depiction is not endorsement. If it was, no artist would be able to paint inhumane practices, no author could write about them, and no filmmaker could delve into the thorny subjects of our time.

Kathryn's next film, *Detroit*, released in 2017 with a screenplay again written by Mark, explores the 1967 Detroit race riots and police brutality through the eyes of a group of Black Vietnam veterans and musicians staying at the Algiers Motel, as well as two white visitors, who are friends of four of the men. The film takes place in the hours before and during the police raid of the motel. During the raid officers kill two Black men, which they then try to pin on a Black security guard who attempted to quell the violence. While critics and survivors of the police assault mostly praised the film for its historical accuracy, some questioned whether, as a white director, she was able to get into the heads of her Black characters.

Kathryn's cast defended her. Lead actor John Boyega, who played security guard Melvin Dismukes, cited Kathryn's seriousness in approaching her subject matter and the way she listened to and collaborated with her Black actors. Interviewed along with Kathryn on *CBS This Morning*, Anthony Mackie, who also acted in *The Hurt Locker*, praised the "progressive" working environment that she created. In the same interview, Kathryn said she hoped *Detroit*, the only feature film about the Detroit riots in 50 years, would contribute to dialogue and healing in a new era of racial division and police violence against Black communities.

Kathryn has carved a unique place for herself as a woman director in what is generally considered the domain of her male counterparts—tense, high-energy films of conflict, violence, and war. James Cameron told CBS's Lesley Stahl, "I think the idea of war and conflict fascinates her. . . . She also takes pride in the fact that she can outgun the guys." For her part, Kathryn does not want to be seen as a woman director but simply a director seeking to explore life-and-death topics in realistic and complex ways, using all the artistic and cinematic means available to her. Even so, as she said in the same interview on the eve of her Academy Award triumph, "The journey for women . . . it's a long journey."

Part II
Striving for Diversity:
Generation X Directors

Ava DuVernay: Telling the Stories That Matter

Standing in the hot fields of Louisiana, camera crews are in position waiting to hear "action" while the director speaks to her actors reviewing the last scene take. Ava DuVernay is on the set of her show *Queen Sugar*. For Ava, becoming a pioneering, groundbreaking Black woman filmmaker wasn't the original plan. Before becoming a highly sought after and critically acclaimed director in Hollywood, Ava grew up in Lynwood, a suburb of Los Angeles, California. While Ava did not come from a family that was connected to the industry, she had something more powerful in her arsenal.

In a shared bedroom with her younger sister, Jina, Ava and her sister would create film sets using their imaginations and the items in their home. They split the room in half and created makeshift houses and cars out of cardboard boxes. Their

Barbie dolls were the actors of these shows, while the sisters served as the costume designers, screenwriters, directors, and set designers. "My mom would go to work, come back on a Saturday, and we were still playing on the floor," Ava described. Little did she know that her Saturday morning playtime would help lay the foundation for her future career as one of the most recognizable film directors and prolific storytellers to date in Hollywood.

To help further her love of storytelling and her creative energy, Ava's beloved Aunt Denise introduced Ava to the artistic world. The pair shared a tight bond, despite Aunt Denise being unmarried and without children of her own. By trade Aunt Denise was a registered nurse who worked at night, which meant during the day she could spend her time doing and enjoying what she loved the most: the arts. She would take Ava to museums, art exhibits, and concerts, exposing her to a different world where creatives showcased their various talents. "When you walked in [Aunt Denise's] house in Compton, classical music was playing. Folks would yell, 'Turn that sh—down,' and it would be Bach playing. She was really a rare bird." For Ava, family means everything, so when Aunt Denise was diagnosed with stage four cancer, Ava moved her aunt in to live with her—allowing them to create sacred, but final, memories together.

While her aunt helped her fall in love with the arts, Ava's mother stressed the importance of being a kind human. "My mother would often tell us to treat other people how we want to be treated. That really stuck with me as I grew up." This lesson played out before her eyes one day while having breakfast with her family at a local IHOP. While enjoying the meal with her mother and sisters, a naked man came out of the restroom and collapsed on the floor. Instead of shying away from the spectacle unfolding before them or even passing judgment on the man, her mother covered the man up with her own coat and stayed with the gentleman until help came. As Jina shared, "No manager did that, no employee did that." Her mother's simple action showed a young Ava how to be compassionate to her fellow human. That small gesture laid the foundation for her kindness, generosity, and advocacy for others. This type of philosophy can be seen and felt on her film and television sets.

Before becoming a sought-after director, Ava toyed with the idea of being an attorney. However, when she entered college at the University of California, Los Angeles (UCLA), she majored in English and African American studies. While there, she ventured into broadcast journalism and scored a highly coveted internship at the television network CBS. She imagined at the time that she would produce high-profile news stories and travel around the world seeking to bring awareness of injustices happening elsewhere. As part of her internship, she was assigned to the O. J. Simpson trial. She was tasked to follow a specific juror to gather as much information as she could, and on one occasion, she found herself digging through the trash of that juror. Needless to say, the internship didn't leave the best impression on her, and she decided that broadcast journalism was best left to others.

However, the experience allowed her to be exposed to another side of the entertainment industry—public relations. It was through the CBS internship that she saw firsthand how publicists worked in the entertainment field. After her graduation, she briefly worked for a small public relations firm called the Bender Group. She took the experience from this first public relations gig and began her own firm: the DuVernay Agency. Her entrepreneurial spirit was passed down from the man who raised her and her siblings—Murray Maye (affectionately called Pops)—who owned his own upholstery business while she was growing up. Under the umbrella of her own company, she worked on movies such as *Collateral*, *Invictus*, and *Dream Girls*.

As a public relations officer, she could be on film sets, have a front row seat moviemaking, and rub elbows with studio execs and film crew members. While exploring the different movie sets, she noted a startling issue playing out over and over—most of the people she encountered were white men. The lack of women and people of color was glaring. This inspired Ava to center diversity in hiring for the projects she would later direct, because she knew the power of having an amazing film crew on set.

In 2006 Ava picked up a camera to film her first short film, *Saturday Night Life*, which is based upon her mother's experiences as a young woman. The film lasts 12 minutes and showcases a mother and her three young children on a trip to a local grocery store. This experience gave Ava her first taste at directing, thus opening her eyes and creating a domino effect, setting the stage for her take on more roles behind the camera. Instead of going to school for a degree in filmmaking, she opted to keep learning on her own. She tried her hand at a full-length film with the 2008 documentary *This Is the Life* to get her feet wet. The documentary is set at a café that spotlighted local hip-hop and rap artists. It is where Ava herself had performed as the rapper Eve. It would be another two years before she released her first feature film, *I Will Follow*.

It is often said that life imitates art, and this film was no exception. In 2003 Aunt Denise lost her battle with breast cancer. Ava used the film to explore how grieving family members deal with a loved one's passing. Short on time and money, she shot the film in 11 days with a budget of only $50,000. Even with all these constraints, Ava's love for storytelling only grew.

Fueled by her passion, she became dedicated to furthering her knowledge of the craft. She took lessons from Steven Spielberg, Clint Eastwood, and other film directors, but not directly—yet. In addition to beginning private director classes, she stumbled upon a gold mine of information in the director commentaries that came with film DVDs. "I've watched over

200 DVD commentaries." For Ava, the director commentaries were her film school, and she studied each one to gain more knowledge about the industry and craft. "We as women, you know, are often taught there is one way to achieve. It's the formal route; it's the route these guys have gone."

Once confident she could pursue this new journey, she tackled her next project in 2012, called *Middle of Nowhere*. She entered the film into the 2012 Sundance Film Festival, where she became the first Black woman to win the Directing Award. On the heels of this historic win, Ava went on to direct *Selma*, a movie based on the events that led to the 1965 march in Selma, Alabama, regarding voting rights for African Americans. *Selma* set the stage for Ava to potentially be the first Black woman nominated for Best Director at the Academy Awards. However, that didn't come to pass, even as the film was nominated for Best Picture and won Best Original Song. The film was a huge success for Ava and seemed to get folks within the industry excited about her, but even with the success of *Selma*, Ava still didn't quite breakout how she thought she would—at least not yet. She couldn't understand why she wasn't getting offers from studios asking her to direct their next major hit. Meanwhile, her white male counterparts seemed to be enjoying the benefits of a successful movie launch:

> [Colin Trevorrow] is the whipping boy for all this and he is such a nice guy, but how does [he] go from

'Jurassic World' straight into Star Wars? . . . From the little indie that we both did, sitting side by side at Sundance with our films in 2012, and [he] goes from that to 'Jurassic World' to Star Wars, and I go from [The Sundance Film Festival] to 'Selma,' and there is nothing else on the horizon? That didn't feel good, and that had me in a depressed place. Not depressed, but just desperate."

Not one to wallow in despair, she made a phone call to her good friend Oprah Winfrey, who had produced and starred in *Selma*, to seek her wisdom on what to do next. As Oprah listened on the phone, she took a moment to remind Ava that her perception in this situation mattered most. "Take that desperation energy and put into something productive," Oprah said according to Ava. Oprah reminded Ava that she still had opportunities. Her friend was right: Ava needed to look at things from a different vantage point. Although not quite on a movie set, Ava was in New Orleans looking for places to tape her fresh idea for the Oprah Winfrey Network (OWN), what would soon become the series *Queen Sugar*.

The morning after her call with Oprah, the newly inspired Ava and her crew scouted more locations in New Orleans. While she was busy looking for the best spots to film *Queen Sugar*, a couple important e-mails came into her inbox. One was from Steven Spielberg, gauging her interest in directing a film that would star Lupita Nyong'o, and the other was from Walt Disney Pictures, asking her to direct *A Wrinkle in Time*. Little did Ava know, the universe had been working behind the scenes on her behalf. Though pleasantly surprised when she finally reviewed the e-mails, she was unsure about Disney's offer. "Never heard of it," she mentioned in her podcast interview with Geoff Edgers, regarding *A Wrinkle in Time*.

Even though Spielberg's offer was tempting, she ultimately decided to roll the dice with Disney and direct *A Wrinkle in Time*, which proved to be a significant move for her career. Not only was she given the opportunity to reimagine Madeleine L'Engle's classic book, such as by casting an African American protagonist, but also she received a $100 million budget to shoot the film, the largest budget given by a studio to a Black woman—ever. The pressure was on. She knew that if someone else were behind the lens of the camera, there would be no questions about the person's capability. "All of those guys [white men] . . . can build worlds. Will you respect my world? Me building a planet?"

A Wrinkle in Time was released the same weekend Marvel Studios released *Black Panther*. The competition between the two was stiff, and in the end her movie wasn't as successful as she had hoped. Nonetheless, it was a historical moment, one she hopes will become normal in the coming years for women and people of color in the film industry. It should also be noted that both movies were directed by African Americans and stayed in the top box-office spots, a rare feat in the white-dominated industry.

A Wrinkle in Time

Ava is no stranger to the work of diversifying Hollywood—on the screen and off the screen. When Disney approached her about adapting Madeleine L'Engle's classic, *A Wrinkle in Time*, she realized she was taking a leap of faith, because she'd never done a sci-fi film in her career as a director or writer.

The movie was off the beaten path for Ava, who up until that point had only done projects that centered around social justice and activism. The target audience of 8-to-12-year-olds would also be different for her. In addition, the adaptation from book to film would be challenging because the protagonist, Meg Murry, doesn't confront a typical villain and there were no epic battle scenes to be played out on the big screen like in superhero movies. Instead, young Meg, who is searching for her father who had mysteriously disappeared, faces a brain as the bad guy. "The villain is the darkness inside of you," Ava shared with *New York Times*. She continued, "There's no Darth Vader, no battle scene. Her action is progressive, and it's internal." Being able to move that prose into movie format was a mountain, but one that Ava, who was not a stranger to adversity, was willing to scale. "That's why I frigging did it, because it was hard," Ava declared.

With the backing of Disney, Ava set off to cast her film according to her vision. In talking with Jeffrey Brown at PBS, she said, "I'm conscious of the fact that there hasn't been a hero, kind of a cinematic leading lady who's the heroine of her own story, that's been in the body of a black girl. And so to have the opportunity, with Disney's blessing, to say, let's expand this and make sure that all kinds of kids can see themselves in the film . . . I'm proud of that." Ava allowed that sentiment to carry her through the making of the film, reminding herself that the movie was a vehicle to make sure that children from all backgrounds could see themselves as a hero. This was something that Oprah Winfrey said was unheard of back in her early days in television and as a child. "I grew up in an era where there was absolutely zero, minus, images [of Black girls]," she said. "So I do imagine, to be a brown-skinned girl of any race throughout the world, looking up on that screen and seeing Storm, I think that is a capital A, capital W, E, some, AWESOME, experience," Oprah gushed to the *New York Times*' Melena Ryzik.

As with many of her projects, the film took on a more personal tone when a family tragedy struck: the man who raised her as his own, known affectionately as Pops, passed away suddenly from a brief illness a few weeks before Ava started production. His death was similar to the distressing disappearance of Meg's dad in the film. Pops's passing allowed her to remain humble and focused on the tasks before her. It helped her realize that what matters more than her being the first woman of color to lead a $100 million project are the children—especially Black and Brown children—who will see the film and hopefully see the hard work she put into creating this project.

Although *A Wrinkle in Time* was different from her previous works, such as *Selma*, it still required her to tap into a space in which underrepresented communities are at the forefront. "Civil rights work and social justice work take imagination, to imagine a world that isn't there, and imagine that it can be there. And that's the same thing that you do whenever you imagine and insert yourself in a future space, or in a space where you've been absent."

But even with all these successes in Ava's professional life, the world around her was still filled with social injustice against Black men and women. "An artist and an activist are not so far apart." She grew up during the era of Daryl Gates as the chief of police for the Los Angeles police Department (LAPD). Gates was well known for having helicopters hover around the city, developing the country's first Special Weapons and Tactical (SWAT) unit, and helping to start the Drug Abuse Resistance Education (DARE) programs. But for all the good he attempted to bring to the City of Angels, Black and Brown people often suffered harsh consequences and treatment. "Living in it you don't discuss it," Ava recalls. "It's just the fabric of the neighborhood. But it's clear that it was wrong and an oppressive environment."

Frustrated with what she was seeing on the news, Ava wanted her storytelling to help bring awareness of social justice issues to the masses. In 2017 it was announced that she would create what would be the Emmy-winning and critically acclaimed limited television series *When They See Us*. The series brings a powerful and relevant narrative to the forefront, detailing the story of the five falsely accused Black and Brown boys known as the Central Park Five: Korey Wise, Kevin Richardson, Raymond Santana, Antron McCray, and Yusef Salaam.

On April 19, 1989, a jogger named Trisha Meili was running through the park when she was brutally attacked. The Central Park Five—who at the time of the attack were between the ages of 14 and 16—had been singled out as the perpetrators of the horrific incident. One of the boys, Korey Wise, who was not an official suspect at the time, found himself facing criminal charges when he went with Yusef to show moral support. The NYPD had a serious issue on their hands with people being mugged at dusk in Central Park at that time. Specifically, on the night in question, there had been more than 30 teenagers in the park, and at least 8 other people in addition to Trisha were hurt that same evening. Something had to be done—even if that meant arresting five boys and getting a conviction based on coerced confessions and faulty eyewitness testimony.

In 2002 the convictions of all the Central Park Five, now men, were vacated when Matias Reyes confessed to the attack of Trisha and his DNA was matched to the evidence of the crime. Although the city of New York denied any wrongdoing in their prosecution of the men, it settled a civil suit with them in the amount of $41 million. In 2019 Ava released the four-part series on Netflix entitled *When They See Us*, retelling in vivid detail that fateful night and the ensuing events.

But prior to her releasing *When They See Us*, in 2016, she directed one of the most significant documentaries regarding mass incarceration, entitled *13th*—aptly named for the 13th Amendment of the US Constitution. The Netflix documentary explores how the amendment still operates as a tool to continue slavery through the mass incarceration of Black people, especially men.

The History of the 13th Amendment

Slavery in the United States was a huge economic driver, especially for Southern states. In fact, a four-year battle began as a result of rising tensions between the Northern and Southern states regarding the institution of slavery. When Abraham Lincoln was elected president of the then United States on November 6, 1860, his win set off a firestorm among the Southern states. He was a member of the newly formed Republican Party and ran largely on an antislavery platform, furthering the dissent among his opposers. His presidency served as the catalyst for South Carolina, Mississippi, Georgia, Florida, Alabama, Louisiana, and Texas to break off from the Union and form the Confederate States of America. They were soon followed by North Carolina, Tennessee, Virginia, and Arkansas. Lincoln claimed that he had no intentions of ending slavery where it was legal or repealing the Fugitive Slave Act of 1850 and that his focus would remain on keeping the Union together. Still, his words were not well received by the people and instead horrified African Americans and his supporters who were against slavery. In April 1861 the Civil War began when the Confederate army attacked Fort Sumter in Charleston, South Carolina, which was a federal stronghold.

Lincoln would waver back and forth over the years regarding his stance on slavery. He insisted that the war was not about slavery nor was it about giving Black Americans equality. Most northern white people were not interested in seeing African Americans become freed men and women and thus had no interest in fighting a war that involved that cause. According to PBS, "For this reason, the government turned away African American volunteers who rushed to enlist. Lincoln upheld the laws barring blacks from the army, proving to northern whites that their race privilege would not be threatened." However, Lincoln eventually started to allow Blacks to fight in the war. There was even a point when enslaved Blacks who had escaped, then called "fugitive slaves," were considered contraband and would be set free by the Union if it was found that their labor had helped the Confederate soldiers in any way. However, the war was still going strong, and Lincoln was running out of ideas. The Confederate states were using enslaved African Americans to aid them in the war, and there was news that Europe would recognize the Confederate states if Lincoln didn't declare that the war was indeed about freeing the slaves. So, he drafted a Emancipation Proclamation.

In a risky move, he threatened the Confederacy with the legislation that, in short, would free all the enslaved people in the areas deemed as rebel states if they refused to surrender and accept defeat. The proclamation was issued after the Union secured a major victory against the Confederate army in September 1862 and thus sent a warning to all those states that any remaining slaves would be free on January 1, 1863. While slavery would end in the rebel states, the proclamation failed to address the

1 million enslaved people in the Union state territories and would leave them in bondage.

Still, the two sides of the country battled against each other until April 1865. At its end, the war had claimed an estimated 617,000 American lives, injured thousands more, and left the entire country in shambles. To date, this is still the bloodiest war fought in American history. On April 14, 1865, Lincoln was assassinated by a Confederate sympathizer, John Wilkes Booth—eight months before the 13th Amendment* was ratified by Congress, officially abolishing and prohibiting slavery at the federal level.

It was 151 years after the Civil War when Netflix released Ava's documentary *13th*, which goes into great detail about the history of the amendment and how it has been applied in the modern day. Throughout the documentary, various experts make the case that the amendment has been used as a tool to control Black and Brown people through its language, specifically, the words between the commas: *except as a punishment for crime whereof the party shall have been duly convicted.* For Ava, sharing this information was her way to connect "two different

---

*Amendment XIII (1865)
Section 1. Neither slavery nor involuntary servitude, except as a punishment for crime whereof the party shall have been duly convicted, shall exist within the United States, or any place subject to their jurisdiction.
Section 2. Congress shall have power to enforce this article by appropriate legislation.
("Constitution of the United States," United States Senate, https://www.senate.gov/civics/constitution_item/constitution.htm#amdt_13_(1865).)

kinds of audiences—folks out there that know about this and folks out there that have never heard of it." The documentary further explores how mass incarceration has become a profitable business within the United States. According to the statistics mentioned in the documentary, "the US accounts for 5% of the world's population, but 25% of its population in prisoners."

However, in true Ava fashion, her purpose behind creating the documentary was to remind people that Black joy is real and that Black culture is more than the hurt, pain, and trauma that systemic racism has passed down from generation to generation. "Black trauma is not our life," Ava shared in her interview with *USA Today*. "We are survivors, as many different kinds of people are."

Ava is a force in Hollywood and is opening doors for traditionally underrepresented communities, especially women of color—not only on set but off set as well. The early lessons she learned from her mother helped cultivate her approach to creating a work environment that others want to join. For example, she has implemented "a no asshole rule." She says, "If a star has to be coddled, then my set is probably not the best one for them." She is also known for hiring a diverse set of crew members for her projects. She makes it a point to treat everyone equally, from the highest-profile actors to the key grip on set, emphasizing the fact that no person is better than another because of their status. She is in many ways a rare bird, like her aunt Denise, in Hollywood.

Regina King: Making Queen Moves

Most childhood actors fade from the spotlight and usually end up on an episode of *Where Are They Now?* But Regina Rene King's career spans over three decades, and she's only beginning to scratch the surface of her Hollywood career. Born in the Golden State of California on January 15, 1971, Regina is the oldest of two girls. With the support of her mother, she started taking acting classes with the legendary Betty Bridges, until she got her big break. At 13 years old, she was cast to play Brenda on the popular NBC show *227*.

Despite Regina's newfound fame, her mother kept her grounded. She knew that it was important for Regina to stay rooted in her values and morals. "My mom told NBC . . . I wasn't going to one of those Hollywood private schools. I was staying in public school," she said in an interview with *People* magazine.

When *227* ended in 1990, Regina headed off to the University of Southern California (USC) to study communications. "Acting was a hobby for me when I started out, or maybe it was because there weren't a lot of examples of me when I found an interest in this art form," she shared in an interview with *Vulture*. After two years at USC, Regina took a leap of faith and dropped out of school to pursue acting full time. The first movie role she auditioned for was in the new John Singleton film, *Boyz n the Hood*. Regina tried and got the role of Shalika, the girlfriend of rapper Ice Cube's character. She took her success with this part as a sign that she had made the right decision in leaving school to pursue acting. "It needed to happen that way so I could say, 'Okay, this is good for you, and you're supposed to be an actor.'"

However, after landing parts in John Singleton's next two movies, *Poetic Justice* and *Higher Learning*, Regina noticed a disturbing pattern in the characters she was playing. "I saw that a lot of us were being stereotyped. I didn't want to be part of that—that's not the narrative I was creating for myself." While grateful for the roles that came, Regina wasn't cool with being labeled as the loudmouth sidekick. She did not want to feed a negative point of view of Black women or be known for such roles in her acting career. Regina understood her worth and knew the power in her saying no when Hollywood tried to keep her in a box. Regina refused to be limited and waited patiently for the right role that would show the depth of her acting talent. Besides, if she couldn't connect to the characters that were being presented to her and give the role depth by creating a backstory, then it wasn't the role for her.

Then in 1996 an opportunity presented itself by way of the movie *Jerry Maguire,* starring Tom Cruise. The casting director was seeking a strong actor to play Marcee Tidwell, the wife of Rod Tidwell (played by Cuba Gooding Jr.). This was the moment in her career she had been waiting for. This character, Marcee, was a dynamic woman who was super protective of her husband's football career and of her family. This role offered Regina a way out the box that Hollywood wanted to keep her in.

Regina changed her manager and agent, and she credits the shift in her career to her new team, who sought all types of roles for her, regardless of whether the writer had a Black actor in mind for the part. As she shared with NPR, "The good news for me is that I have an amazing team behind me, and they've been with me for 20 years now—almost 20 years. And they have seen me as an actress, not necessarily just a black actress. So, I have been lucky enough for them to see me that way."

After the success of *Jerry Maguire,* Regina's star power rose. However, her main responsibility was to her son. Any parts she took going forward had to be worth her time—especially if she was going to be away from him for an extended period. "I'm not missing out on his life," she said. "I don't ever want my son to say, 'Well, the nanny was there.' I would be devastated."

But soon she found herself working behind the camera. She was approached by R&B singer Jahiem about being in his musical video for "Finding My Way Back." Flattered, she agreed to be in his video but with one condition: she would direct the video. Jahiem knew she could act, but he didn't know if she could do what is required of directors, such as creating a treatment—an extremely detailed outline of a media project. Not one to back down from a challenge, she got the learning to make good on her word.

One Night in Miami

Muhammad Ali, Malcom X, Jim Brown, and Sam Cooke all came together on the night of February 25, 1964, in Miami, after Muhammad Ali, still Cassius Clay at the time, had a fight against Sonny Liston. Muhammad had gone into the fight as the underdog. However, he won and proved himself to be the true heavyweight champion of the world. After the fight that evening, the four men met up at the popular Hampton House—a hot spot for Black celebrities—where the conversation details are unknown but are assumed to be about the current state of the civil rights movement and of the Black community as a whole. While the contents of the meeting are undetermined, one outcome was that the name Cassius Clay was no longer, replaced with Muhammad Ali.

One Night in Miami. . ., which was released on Amazon Prime in 2020, marked Regina's feature-film directorial debut. Before Regina turned it into a film, *One Night in Miami* was a play written by Kemp Powers, who had researched the evening between the four men and created dialogue based on their personalities. In 2019 Regina got her hands on the play's script and the screenplay, which Kemp had also written. After reading both scripts, she knew that she had to tell the story of these prolific men and help bring Kemp's vison to life. Regina said to the *New York Times*' Salamishah Tillet, "I also thought Kemp's words were a love letter to the Black man's experience. As an audience member, I feel like I don't often get the opportunity to see our men realized onscreen the way we see them in real life."

Regina saw this as an opportunity to tell her truth and bring it to power on the silver screen. The subject of the movie dealt with the same racial injustices that are still happening today. The year 2020 was not only the first of the COVID-19 pandemic but also a year when several injustices were committed against Black people, most notably the murders of Breonna Taylor, George Floyd, and

Ahmaud Arbery. "This subject has been present for Black people ever since our history in America has existed," Regina said, referring to the civil rights issue in America. The film went on to earn three Oscar nominations: Best Supporting Actor (Leslie Odom Jr.), Best Adapted Screenplay (Kemp Powers), and Best Original Song (Leslie Odom Jr. and Sam Ashworth)—not bad for an actor debuting as film director.

Her direction of the music video was a huge success—so much so that director Paris Barclay suggested that she join a broadcast-network directing program. "He said it would help people take me more seriously as a director if they know I was actively pursuing learning about it, outside of what I picked up being on set as an actor," Regina shared. She decided to enter ABC's directing program, which at the time was under the leadership of Shonda Rhimes. Because of her experience as an actor, Regina brought a unique flair and creative eye to the sets that she took over. She also knew how best to work with her fellow actors and provide direction to them on scenes.

But Regina's career shift also came with a reduction in pay. "It's tough, because you don't make as much as a director in the beginning stages as you do as an actor. . . . It's truly something I'm doing because I'm passionate about it. I'm making the choice to carve out the time."

Over the years Regina—whose name in Latin means "queen"—has amassed several awards for her acting. The past 30 years have been filled with ups and downs, but she always remained persistent and consistent. She has found new ways to challenge herself—whether its voicing characters on *The Boondocks*, playing a Muslim American, or standing behind the camera giving direction to her fellow actors. She knows no bounds when it comes to taking control over her career. Regina reigns supreme in everything she touches.

Shonda Rhimes:
The Titan of Television

"Don't you have enough?" This question was allegedly asked of Shonda Rhimes by a high-ranking executive at ABC. Taken aback by this query to her request for an additional ticket for her sister to go Disneyland, Shonda decided in that moment to leave ABC after working there for 15 years and to take her talents to Netflix. The move was shocking to those within the television industry to say the least, but Shonda knew that she needed to be in a place that celebrated her, knew her worth, and would let her authentic, creative self thrive without restrictions.

During her time with ABC, which is owned by Disney, Shonda was responsible for over 70 hours of programing for the network, earning herself millions of dollars and the network $2 billion from her various shows. She dubbed herself a titan because nobody in television was doing the same caliber of work as she was. She even created a production company aptly named Shondaland. Her creative brain is global, and at one time people around the world were brought into her artistic mind and the various worlds she created through her shows. During her time at ABC, she had three (and sometimes even four) shows—*Grey's Anatomy*, *Scandal*, and *How to Get Away with Murder*—in production. With this many shows running, her wheel of creativity was constantly turning.

Shonda's vivid imagination has been brewing since she was a child playing in her family's pantry with the soup cans. But it was her ability to lie, or tell stories—it's been said both ways—that helped to fuel her love of storytelling. But don't pass too much judgment on her; it is her job, after all, to create believable worlds for television. "I make up stuff because I have to," she shares in her bestselling memoir. "Imagining is now my job. I write television shows. I make up characters. I create whole worlds in my head. . . . I wrap myself in fiction. Fiction is my job. Fiction is it. Fiction is everything. Fiction is my jam," she unashamedly admits.

Years before Shonda courageously left ABC, she had another moment of reflection during Thanksgiving dinner with her family. As she and her older sister were helping make dinner, her sister playfully challenged her with six words: "You never say yes to anything." Now Shonda wasn't afraid of a challenge, but did her big sister know who she was talking to? This is the woman who reminded her audience a few times in her highly watched TED talk that she is responsible for several hours' worth of programming with at least $350 million budgeted between all her shows. She is a busy woman. Her *yes* must be selective and well thought out. Sometimes a no is necessary. However, that simple statement from her big sister served as the catalyst for Shonda to be more open to using the word *yes*. She decided that for all of 2014, she would say yes to everything that made her afraid. Within one year she discovered that saying that three-letter word changed her world for the best.

As if on cue, the universe started sending her largest fears her way. Shonda has a fear of public speaking? The president of her Ivy League alma mater, Dartmouth College, asks her to do the commencement speech for the June 2014 graduating class. She's afraid of being on television? The folks at *Jimmy Kimmel Live!* give her a ring to see if *this* time works for her. Yup, it does. Her youngest daughter wants to play before Shonda heads out to a fancy dinner with friends? Not a fear, but definitely yes!— but only after much hesitation over wrinkling her ball gown and playing with her daughter's sticky little hands.

"Wanna play?" her baby girl, Emerson, asked Shonda one day when she was preparing to head out for a formal event. As Shonda noted in her book, *Year of Yes: How to Dance It Out, Stand in the Sun and Be Your Own Person*, it wasn't so much the question that took her off guard as much as it was her daughter not using her usual *honey* before requests, dropping the quirk that had always made Emerson sound like a southern waitress. It was in that moment Shonda realized that her baby girl was changing before her eyes. As much she wanted to say no to playing so as to not be late, Shonda found it hard to turn Emerson down, who wanted to spend a few moments with her mommy.

Shonda describes a hum that she normally experienced as she worked. But in the busy stresses of her life, the hum had somehow gotten lost along the way. Her creative flow seemed to dwindle as she kept pushing forward with new shows, and it felt as if she was going through the motions and the work was no longer as fun as it used to be. She started to wonder: Had she reached her creative cap? Was she beginning to plateau? As she shares in her TED talk, "My Year of Saying Yes to Everything," the hum was tied not only to her writing but also to all the moving parts involved with being a showrunner.

But in those fifteen minutes she played with her daughter, she discovered her hum had come back. She recognized that she had been missing a vital piece of the puzzle: play. The year of yes was less about saying yes to the big events than it was about saying yes to the smaller life events—the moments in life that are easily glossed over or can be explained away with a "mommy has to go to work" or a "can I get a rain check, friend? I got this script to crank out." Shonda understood her worth is not tied to what she is creating for a television network but is tied to the people around her—her children, family, and friends. Because without their love, support, and guidance, would she really be a titan?

Before Shonda made the final decision to leave ABC, she sat down to meet with Netflix executive Ted Sarandos. One of the first things she let him know was that she wasn't interested in recreating shows she had made for ABC on Netflix. She wanted "to be in a place where I can make stuff and no one's going to bother me or make me feel like I'm beholden," she shared with Lacey Rose at the *Hollywood Reporter* regarding her conversation with Ted. She needed to be somewhere where she would be celebrated, not tolerated.

After her conversation with Ted about coming over to Netflix, Shonda toyed with the idea of leaving ABC but decided to put a pause on it. After all, how could she leave the place that had propelled her to a type of stardom rarely seen among showrunners? Fans are usually invested in the world created by the director, screenwriter, or showrunner, but they rarely know the name behind that world. However, a quick pass through Shonda's Twitter feed will give a snapshot of the reactions of angry fans when they learn that a beloved character is killed off or won't be returning to their favorite show. Shonda has reached fame—unintentionally or not—and is a household name.

However, this popularity didn't seem to help with the contract negotiations with her soon-to-be-former job at ABC. Despite being able to bring in over $2 billion for its parent company, Disney, Shonda still found herself having to fight with them about episode details, about more money for herself and staff, and even over a commercial she had produced in support of a US presidential candidate. Her creativity was stifled in all the constant back and forth with the network. "I felt like I was dying . . . like I'd been pushing the same ball up the same hill in the exact same way for a really long time." Shonda was tired of fighting, and after the network executive pushed back on her simple request, it was time to move on from ABC and start a new chapter with Netflix.

After signing her deal with the streaming company, Shonda found herself with a unique problem. She didn't have any new show ideas, which was unusual for her. As she shared with the *New York Times*, "It wasn't like I had a treasure trove of ideas in the back of my head that I'd been hiding and saving. So the panic overtook me for a while." But a trip away from the ever-busy Los Angeles to peaceful Arizona would prove to be the cure she needed to get her creative juices flowing again.

One of the many things Shonda does well is take an actual story from the news and put her own unique spin on it. Take, for example, *Grey's Anatomy*—which at this time of this book is the longest-running prime-time medical drama, surpassing its predecessor, *ER*, with currently no signs of stopping. *Grey's Anatomy* has allowed everyday people to see themselves represented on television. It is not uncommon for fans to share stories about how they or their children have become medical doctors because of the show, or how they have been able to help get a loved one properly diagnosed due to an episode. So when she stumbled across an article about Anna Delvey—a grifter in New York—she knew that she had found her next big show idea for Netflix. "I knew exactly what the show was," she shared excitedly with the *New York Times*. With a newfound creative energy flowing through her, Shonda thought up seven more show ideas for Netflix.

The *Bridgerton* Phenomenon

Romance novels are dreamy, so it's no surprise that they often make for great movies and television shows. Set in 19th-century England, the Bridgerton series follows a group of eight siblings and explores their different paths to love.

While the stories in the books are amazing, it's how Shonda stumbled onto these books that's the real happily ever after. Julia Quinn, the author of the historical romance series, was hanging out at a Starbucks doing what most people do while drinking a hot mocha latte—pretending to work—when she got the call that changed her life. As she shared on the *Tamron Hall Show*, "The way I understand it, Shonda ran out of books to read on vacation and somehow stumbled on one of mine."

It's 1837 in England, and it is time for of-age maidens to enter womanhood and become wives. For young Daphne Bridgerton, who she selects for a husband is key for her future. After all, some little girls dream of weddings and babies. Enter Simon Bassett, the Duke of Hastings, a handsome Black man—wait, what? A duke that is Black? A queen that is Black? Black royals in Regency England? This could only be a Shondaland production.

With one look at any of Shonda's shows, a viewer will immediately notice the abundance of diversity among the cast and even behind the camera. However, Shonda is not a fan of the word *diverse*. As the star of *Scandal*, Kerry Washington, described in *Entertainment Weekly*, Shonda believes in normalizing the world as is and not using differences, such as race or sexual orientation, as a plot point to move a show forward. "When you're the only woman in the room, or the only person over 40, or the only LGBTQ person, you don't get to enter into conversations about what that looks like. But when we *normalize* that combination, then we get to explore what difference means and how it feels and how it lives in the world." Kerry said.

So it should come as no surprise to anyone that Shonda would take a period piece and take creative liberties to ensure the cast reflects the everyday world of her audiences. There is power in pulling together a cast of marginalized characters into the homes of over 82 million Netflix subscribers, putting into action the mantra of "representation matters."

Leaving something familiar is never easy. It can be a hard decision. But there are moments when taking a leap of faith will propel a person to a better position. "I don't know how you do things without betting on yourself," Shonda said in an interview with *Forbes*. "If I was going to play it safe, I would've stayed exactly where I was and kept doing exactly what I was doing. It wasn't like a crazy leap to believe in myself."

Shonda's storytelling extends beyond any television network or streaming service. No matter where she goes, Shonda will always be a titan to reckon with in Hollywood. While some may ask if she has enough, she may very well remind them that only *she* can determine when enough is enough.

Mara Brock Akil

Mara Brock Akil is a dazzling showrunner, a prolific storyteller, and a force within the television industry. A month before the 20th anniversary of her iconic show *Girlfriends*, Mara inked a deal with Netflix to create original content for the platform, joining the ranks with her colleague Shonda at the powerhouse streaming service.

Like Shonda, Mara is well known for her ability to create riveting television shows with memorable characters who tackle real-life issues that help her audiences feel seen. She entered the television scene almost three decades ago as a writer. One of the many strengths Mara has brought to writers' rooms is the ability to tackle complex issues among Black people and humanize those experiences. Her name was seen in the credits of several shows before she ventured to create four shows of her own—*Girlfriends*, *The Game*, *Being Mary Jane*, and *Love Is*.

Born in California but raised in Kansas City, Missouri, Mara originally attended Northwestern University in Chicago to become a journalist. Although there is a strong aspect of storytelling in journalism, Mara soon realized that she wanted to share stories from a different viewpoint, one that allowed more creative perspective. "I really appreciate learning the who, what, when, where, but it's the why," she said. "I'm gonna tell the truth through fiction. And it allows me to when I go exploring why a character is this way."

With her journalism background, Mara set off to forge her own path and entered the Hollywood space in 1994. After a brief writing stint at Fox creating content for the short-lived show *South Central*, she moved over to the United Paramount Network and started writing for the hit show *Moesha*, starring the singer Brandy. She worked on *Moesha* for four years. Under the mentorship of the show's creator, Ralph Farquhar, Mara was able to set into motion her vision for future shows. "I naturally give the best of who I am to those who are around me because the best was given to me, and I think it's important to talk about legacy, not just what I did for others, but who Ralph Farquhar, Sara Finney-Johnson, Vida Spears are, and what they did for me."

It is this belief in pouring into others that led her to do the same for those who came behind her. She even worked with two of her girlfriends to create a scholarship for film students who were interested in telling Black stories.

Mara wasn't afraid to create complex Black characters. She didn't believe in writing stories that put out only positive images or only negative images. She instead focused on the whole person, because real people don't operate in a single dimension. Mara faced criticism, often from other Black people, for writing multidimensional Black characters with challenging story lines. Mara shared, "And what it does is it keeps a lot of artists stuck. That's a burden. That is not an honor to ask me as a creator to rewrite what was wrong in the first place. It's almost validating them. And it shouldn't be our responsibility as Black creators. That's not my responsibility."

While getting nice deals with Netflix is amazing, the most incredible thing that Mara has done in her time in television is cultivate upcoming writers by providing opportunities similar to what she had. She is aware of her status within the industry, and she is proud to have been able to help others rise up in the rankings as well.

Gina Prince-Bythewood: Basketball Courts and Old Guards

Rejection is never easy to accept. However, how a person decides to handle rejection allows them to write their narrative on their own terms. At three weeks old, Gina Maria Prince-Bythewood was placed for adoption by her teenage mother. Growing up in Pacific Grove, California, with her white adoptive family, she didn't see a lot of Black faces that looked like her. And being biracial—white and Black—meant that she wasn't able to connect with one half of herself. As she reminisced about her childhood days, Gina recounted how active her imagination was and how much she loved writing stories. But her parents thought—or hoped—it was a phase. "She kept talking about being a soap opera writer, which was the worst thing to me because I detested soap operas," her mother said in an interview with the *Monterey Herald*.

Even though her parents were not initially on board with her dream of becoming a soap opera writer, Gina never lost the passion for it. She knew what it meant to stand up for herself and go after what she wanted. Giving up, after all, is not how you become the first girl to play on her school's kickball team. "There were no girls' leagues," Gina said. "Boys often didn't want me and my sisters out there," she shared with the Associated Press.

Refusing to take no for an answer proved rewarding. Gina landed a spot in the competitive film school at University of California, Los Angeles, and earned her first writing job on NBC's hit sitcom *A Different World*, which propelled her to write and direct her own movies. "It's so much about ambition and stamina and outworking everybody," she said. "That mentality drives who I am as a director. And this industry early on was constantly telling me that my stories weren't worthy or valid. I kept having to fight for my space."

With that fighting spirit, Gina wanted to challenge the lack of diversity among the faces featured on the big and small screens. It is important to her that films have Black women and women of color prominently featured as the lead, or at the very least, in a significant role in her productions.

She received the opportunity to do that with her first feature film, *Love & Basketball*, which was released in movie theaters in the spring of 2000. Gina became inspired to write this movie after she saw *When Harry Met Sally* in the late 1980s. She wanted not only to create a love story where the main characters were Black but also to shine a light on a character rarely seen in love stories. Gina shared at the 2021 Tribeca Festival, "I wanted to see myself reflected. And then I started wanting to tell the story of this girl that I felt hadn't been seen as well, an athlete."

As with many creative endeavors, this project featured parts of Gina's real life. Like her protagonist Monica, Gina played basketball in high school and college. She also based the love story on her own relationship with her husband, director Reggie Bythewood. Art imitated life. "This was a very personal story. My first kiss was 10 seconds, not five, but we did count on our fingers. So it's fun to pull stuff like that from your life." Gina believed that it was important to have her first movie be somewhat self-representative as she decided to fully step into filmmaking and introduced Hollywood to her style of creating movies.

But before she could make the film and get it into theaters, she had to convince studio executives that it was a story worth telling. At every turn she was met with a resounding no. Most of the studios felt that the story was quiet and didn't provide any real drama. In an interview with the *Hollywood Reporter*, she recounted, "I remember one specific studio suggested that I put in a scene like in *Soul Food* where the wife is chasing her husband with a knife."

With nobody willing to finance the film, the project was as good as dead. However, little did she know that a couple of folks had been discussing her script with the Sundance Institute. Suddenly the project had been revived! Through her partnership with Sundance, Gina was able to receive valuable feedback on her script and connect with producers as well. One of these producers was Spike Lee, who had his own production company, 40 Acres and a Mule Filmworks, and decided to back *Love & Basketball*. The film was created for an estimated $20 million but only earned about $27 million—despite receiving warm reviews from both fans and critics.

It would be eight years after the making of *Love & Basketball* until Gina got to work on her next project, *The Secret Life of Bees*. During that time, she spent time raising her two sons, helping her husband with his own project, and developing a couple of her own projects that didn't pan out. And although she received various scripts after her success with *Love & Basketball*, she didn't feel as if she could take just anything presented to her. "You still felt that as a black director, you had to prove yourself even harder, no matter what people were saying about this great renaissance of black film," she said in an interview with the *New York Times*.

Three years after the release of *Love & Basketball*, she set her sights on adapting Wally Lamb's book *I Know This Much Is True*. In a letter to the author, she shared with him her experiences of growing up with a sibling with mental health challenges. It was this level of transparency and vulnerability that impressed Wally and allowed him to trust her vision to bring the book to the big screen. However, Gina hit a wall when it came to casting the leads for the movie. No matter how hard she attempted to recruit A-list actors for the film, none of them would work on the film because Gina hadn't done enough films for them to want to take a chance. "That was painful, I have to say," Gina admitted. She knew she could do the job, but getting others to see that she was the right person was difficult and frustrated her. "Of course, there's comfort in a director who has done six or seven films, but that doesn't make them any more talented, just more experienced. [The actors] were walking away from what could be a great experience just because of the number of films I'd done."

Although Gina was disappointed with not moving forward with *I Know This Much Is True*, she moved on to the next project. In 2001 Gina received an advance copy of Sue Monk Kidd's book *The Secret Life of Bees*, before it was quite ready for the public. At the time, Gina had finished an adaptation of Terry McMillian's *Disappearing Acts* and was exhausted. And she wasn't immediately in love with the manuscript for *The Secret Life of Bees*.

Then, in 2005, she had lunch with two of the former stars of *Love & Basketball*, Sanaa Lathan and Alfre Woodard. She discovered that they had auditioned for *The Secret Life of Bees*, which at the time was in the hands of another director and seemed to be progressing. Feelings of dread and jealousy overcame her, and she said to herself, "Wait, I should be doing that movie." After her lunch with the ladies, she went home and found the tossed manuscript. This time, she allowed herself to be fully brought into the world that the author, Sue, had created, and Gina finished reading the book in one sitting. Now she really felt terrible for passing on the chance to direct the movie five years ago. "God, I've blown it. I've lost my chance."

But as fate would have it, two months later, the director of the movie dropped out, and another studio, Fox Searchlight, took over the project. The new studio asked Gina if she would be interested in coming on board as director. This time she jumped at the opportunity. And now she didn't have as much trouble recruiting stellar talent for the film, due to the success of the book and because of her own outstanding reputation within Hollywood circles. The stars even agreed to accept less money in order to get the project filmed.

Adoption and the Bees

Taking place during the height of the civil rights movement, a young white girl, Lily, decides on her 14th birthday to run away with her Black housekeeper, Rosaleen, in order to escape her abusive father. Her mother has been dead for about a decade, and Lily takes what few mementos she has as the pair make their way to a small town in South Carolina that may hold the secrets to her mother's past. Lily and Rosaleen come across a trio of Black bee-keeping sisters, and the two create an elaborate story in order to stay with the sisters.

As Gina combed through the script, she found herself relating to the main character, Lily. As an adoptee, Gina had a lot of unanswered questions and often wondered why she had been given up in the first place. "I wanted to find my birth mother and find out why I was given up. What was wrong with me? What could make a mother give up her child?" Eventually, she reunited with her birth mother, but the euphoric feeling that accompanied the reunion was stifled when she discovered the circumstances of how she was born into the world. "It really messed with my head. How could anything good come out of anything so horrible?" As Gina continued to comb through the lines of the movie, she noted a recurring theme: self-love. At one point in Gina's life—like Lily in the movie—Gina didn't believe she was worth loving. "That was how I felt in my 20's. But now I have been able to come out of that." Gina used her real-life experiences as an adoptee to help convey the whirlwind of emotions portrayed throughout the movie by the cast members.

Once again there would be a gap in Gina's resume after completing *The Secret Life of Bees*. But as she listened to singer-songwriter Alicia Keys sing the lyrics to her song

"Diary," Gina found the inspiration for her next project. "And suddenly I just saw this character and this story in my head, and it was like I was watching this movie while she was singing. And it was just a phenomenal moment. And I just could not wait to get home and put it down."

Driven by her newfound motivation, she got to work writing the script for her next film, *Beyond the Lights*. The first several drafts of the script were filled with personal anecdotes, and she knew she needed to dig deeper. "I love directing, writing is a chore. It's very hard for me. But it all starts with the script. And you have to work it and work it. Writing is really rewriting." Before she knew it, she had rewritten the script 55 times before feeling that she had reached the real drama and intent behind the love story. "It was a love story first set in the music world as opposed to being a music film."

With the script done, she next needed to get the film into studio hands to get the green light for the project. However, more doors slammed in Gina's face, and she struggled to find a home for the movie. With the success of *The Secret Life of Bees*, she believed that getting studio backing would be an easy win. Instead, she encountered pushback that she believed was due to two things: "One was the suicide in it and studios feeling like that made it feel small and that audiences couldn't come back from that. And the other is that there's two people of color at the helm and studios feeling that that's harder to market and makes it a smaller film."

Eventually she found a studio that was willing to option the script for a year. While not a guarantee that the studio would finance the movie, she possibly could stop her search. She began to audition the lead roles for the film. For the female protagonist, she knew she wanted a singer, but one by one, the actors she and the studio wanted didn't work out or didn't fit the vision. But then Gugu Mbatha-Raw auditioned for the lead role. Gina felt an instant connection, just like that night at the Alicia Keys concert. As Gugu started her audition, Gina "saw the film while [Gugu] was talking. It's just a great moment as a director when you know this is the one." However, the studio that was potentially backing the project wasn't on board with her casting a relatively unknown actor as the lead and pulled out from the project altogether. Once again Gina was back at square one.

Still not deterred, she kept going with the project. This time she and Gugu put together an eight-minute presentation showcasing Gugu's talent, in addition to giving potential investors a peek at what the film was about. Things started moving in the right direction when BET agreed to provide $2 million for the film. All she had to do was find a studio. Thinking she had the golden ticket, she went back to those same studios, only to be told no again. She told *Vulture*, "Everyone loved the script, loved me, loved Gugu, but she's not a star. So we thought it was dead again. But then we decided to shoot this independently. I thought, *What am I whining about? Stop asking for permission.*

This is a story I've got to tell, it's stuck in my head. It's driving me crazy, so let me just shoot it." Soon Relativity Media got behind the project and allowed Gina the creative freedom to cast the film as she saw fit.

After the conclusion of *Beyond the Lights* in 2014, it would be another six years before she directed her next film. In 2020 *The Old Guard* was released on Netflix. She told *Indiewire*, "I only do films that I'm absolutely passionate about. To be away from my two boys, my husband, there has to be a really good reason. And it takes me a long time to write. And being a mom. You can't just take off every other year to work on a project."

And *The Old Guard* proved to be a very good reason to spend a little time away from home. With the movie, Gina made history as the first Black woman to direct a comic book movie with a huge eight-figure budget. She was playing in the major leagues now. It was only a few years before the release of *The Old Guard* that Ava DuVernay was the first Black women to direct a high-budget live-action film. Women and especially women of color have a hard time gaining opportunities like this, and Gina knew she couldn't squander this one. Directing and being entrusted with a film of this caliber opened doors for her. This has given her the space to tell the stories that she wants but most importantly to make sure that Black people and other marginalized people are seen—Finally.

Kimberly Peirce: Genderqueer Filmmaker and Activist

In the early morning of December 31, 1993, two men broke into the Humboldt, Nebraska, home where 21-year-old transgender man Brandon Teena, two other adults in their 20s, and a nine-month-old baby were living. In the presence of the child, they shot and killed Brandon and the other adults. The same men had kidnapped Brandon from a Christmas party a week earlier and sexually assaulted him in a vacant lot next to a meatpacking plant. When Brandon reported the assault, the small-town police humiliated him and notified his assailants of the report, an act that made him a marked man and led days later to the triple murder.

At the time of these brutal crimes, Kimberly Peirce lived more than 1,200 miles away in New York City. During the day, she was a film student at Columbia University and at night, a proofreader in a law office to earn money for her studies. Several months after Brandon's murder she read about it in a copy of the *Village Voice* left behind at her office. In that moment, her life changed forever. "I was completely obsessed with telling his story. I didn't know trans people, and the lesbians that I knew didn't know trans people," she later said.

Over the next few years, Kimberly traveled to Lincoln, Nebraska, where Brandon was born, and then to Falls City, where he'd moved to live as a man in a place where no one knew him. She interviewed his friends and family and attended the trial of his murderers. Kimberly's research culminated in an award-winning thesis project in 1995, which then became the 1999 acclaimed feature film *Boys Don't Cry*.

Hilary Swank, who played Brandon in the film, received the Academy Award and the Golden Globe for Best Actress, while Chloë Sevigny, who played Brandon's girlfriend, won a Golden Globe in the supporting actress category. The film itself was nominated for Best Picture and Kimberly for Best Director in her first full-length film. She and her screenplay coauthor, Andy Bienen, won multiple screenwriting awards.

Premiering one year after the murder of the gay University of Wyoming student Matthew Shepard, *Boys* had impact far beyond the screen. It raised public awareness of trans people and the violence they often encountered and helped to expand hate crimes legislation to cover sexual orientation and gender identity.

Hate Crimes Legislation in the United States

In 1968 the US Congress passed the first law against hate crimes, defined as violence or threats of violence against people due to their race, ethnicity, religion, or national origin. These laws grew out of the civil rights movement and the long history of violence against Black people and other people of color. In 2009 the Matthew Shepard and James Byrd Jr. Hate Crimes Prevention Act expanded these protections to gender, gender identity, sexual orientation, and disability. Under these two laws, suspects whose crimes are deemed to be hate crimes face additional federal charges beyond those of arson, assault, murder, or any other state or federal crime with which they are charged. Many states have also passed their own legislation that increases prison terms and other penalties for a hate crime.

Growing up, Kimberly didn't see herself becoming either a filmmaker or an activist for LGBTQI+ rights. Born in Harrisburg, Pennsylvania, on September 8, 1967, she lived briefly in New York City before her family settled in Miami, Florida. To help pay her undergraduate tuition at the University of Chicago, she taught English in Japan for two years and worked as a photographer. Believing photography to be her career path, she interned for the famous photojournalist Alfred Eisenstaedt at *Time* magazine before returning to UChicago to finish her degree.

A class in gender studies made Kimberly change her mind about her future. Captivated by her professor, Lauren Berlant, and the topics covered, she decided to pursue an academic career, conducting research and teaching at the university level. When it came time for her to apply to graduate school, though, Lauren convinced her that her talents lay outside traditional scholarly pursuits; in Kimberly's words, "sometimes, teachers tell you what you're not supposed to do." Lauren praised her understanding of films, and Kimberly ended up applying to graduate school in film—though she later attributed her research and writing skills to her literature and gender studies classes.

During her undergraduate years and in graduate school at Columbia, Kimberly was also exploring her own sexuality and gender identity. In the early 1990s, filmmaking was still a male-dominated field. "I didn't really have people to model myself after—other than Jane Campion. So I modeled myself after the boys," she said.

Growing up in a working-class family in the 1970s and '80s, she experienced physical and sexual violence and tried to fit into the mold of a straight, cisgender girl and woman. Brandon's experiences of violence, his attraction to girls and women, and his "moves to live as a straight guy in a relatively straight world, dating women and being buddies with the guys" spoke to Kimberly's personal feelings and evolution. In film school she also dated women, and she questioned her own relationship to the gender binary.

Being Genderqueer

Kimberly defines herself as genderqueer, which means not conforming to conventional gender distinctions and often being fluid in terms of gender identity. She says,

> Gender identity can be a profound thing for many of us. We may have a gender. We may have multiple genders. Yet, we have a society that suggests there are only two genders, that assigns us one of those two genders and tends to suggest we stay put in the one we are originally assigned to. Society can place expectations on how we, as a "male" or as a "female," should dress, cut our hair, talk, and behave.

While many genderqueer people use pronouns like *they/them/theirs* or newly coined pronouns like *ze* and *zir*, Kimberly currently prefers the pronouns *she/her/hers* that she has used throughout her career.

To Kimberly, *Boys* reflects the experiences of transgender and genderqueer youth who had far less support within the broader culture than young people do today. Brandon had no advice books, no novels depicting trans men, and no real-life role models when he moved 100 miles away, from a city of more than 200,000 people to a town of fewer than 10,000, to start a new life. The film shows the measures he took: binding his chest, wearing men's clothing, and stuffing socks into his jeans. While many trans people today don't receive gender reassignment surgery or hormone therapy, Brandon had no choice. These means were not even available.

Critics praised the movie's realism, attention to detail, and deep understanding of its characters and setting. Calling *Boys* a "stunning debut," Janet Maslin of the *New York Times* wrote, "Ms. Peirce has found a way to tell [Brandon Teena's story] brilliantly, with 'Badlands,' 'Bonnie and Clyde' and 'In Cold Blood' among her inspirations, and with Theodore Dreiser's idea of American tragedy hauntingly reawakened."

Roger Ebert deemed it "one of the best films of the year." He wrote, "The first time I saw the movie, I was completely absorbed by the characters—the deception, the romance, the betrayal. Only later did I fully realize what a great film it is, a worthy companion to those other masterpieces of death on the prairie."

Reviews lauded the performances that Kimberly elicited from her young actors. Hilary Swank, recently fired from popular TV show *Beverly Hills, 90210* and down on her luck, agreed to be paid $75 per day, $3,000 in total, for her work in the leading role that would win her an Oscar and a Golden Globe. To play Brandon, she cut her hair short, lost weight, and lived in public as a man for a month. Chloë Sevigny's performance as

Brandon's girlfriend, Lana Tisdel, received equal praise; Roger Ebert wrote, "although Hilary Swank deserves all praise for her performance as Brandon, it is Sevigny who provides our entrance into the story."

What seemed to be strengths of the film at the time, however, turned out to be controversies in retrospect. To give Brandon's story more focus and intensity and to reduce the number of characters—always a goal in low-budget films because actors must still be paid—Kimberly combined characters, changed names, and eliminated one of the shooting victims altogether. That person was Phillip DeVine, the disabled Black boyfriend of Lana's older sister, also left out of the film. Kimberly has argued that *Boys* is a work of fiction, not a documentary—the documentary *The Brandon Teena Story* was released a year earlier—and she had to make the decisions that best served her story. To activists challenging a white-dominated film industry and that industry's depictions of people in the heartland as all white, Kimberly's leaving Phillip out of the movie was seen as erasing a Black person from the setting and the true story, as well as the racism that likely played a role in his death.

The second controversy had to do with Brandon's girlfriend Lana, who objected to the film's portrayal of her and invasion of her privacy, even though Kimberly had interviewed Lana and her mother to research the film. Again, some of the details had been changed in service of the story, among them the ending in which Brandon dies in Lana's arms. (She was not anywhere near the house at the time of the shooting.) Fox Searchlight Pictures settled Lana's lawsuit in 2000 for an undisclosed amount of money. Despite her objections to her own portrayal, Lana was reported to have praised the film's depiction of Brandon, saying, "She captured the real Brandon."

The third controversy involved Kimberly's casting of cisgender, heterosexual Hilary Swank to play the role of Brandon. After completing her short thesis film at Columbia in 1995, Kimberly spent three years searching for the right actor. She auditioned more than 100 people, including drag kings and trans actors, but she said that none of their performances reflected her vision for Brandon's character. In later interviews, Kimberly cited Hilary's Midwestern roots, her frequent moves and experience of homelessness, and the difficulties she faced trying to fit into her school and community. Kimberly said she wanted "to find somebody who lives the way Brandon does. . . . [Hilary] came the closest to bringing to life the person that we all wanted to bring to life."

Nonetheless, many transgender activists felt that one of their own should have been given this opportunity, which would have raised the visibility and helped the careers of trans actors. Like other actors from marginalized communities, those who identify as LGBTQI+ often see their roles played by outsiders, many of whom do so in inauthentic ways. The claim that no qualified person from the community could be found seemed like one more excuse to maintain an unjust status quo.

Some activists felt the movie's version of Brandon's final week gave too much attention to the brutality and sexual violence he experienced, to which Kimberly responded,

> Given that I'm a survivor of physical and sexual abuse, I am deeply passionate about never creating what I call pornography of violence. I never want to create a situation where you see the person I'm having violence unleashed upon in a way that makes you disrespect that person or makes you want to unleash violence on another human. Every day I shot, I just kept saying to myself, "Am I adding to violence? No. I believe I'm adding to humanity."

Incident at Reed College

These objections culminated in protests against Kimberly at Reed College in Portland, Oregon, when she spoke to a student group in November 2016. The students were already angry and scared because of the unexpected election of Donald Trump several days earlier. They confronted Kimberly about the transphobic violence depicted in *Boys*, the casting of Hilary Swank, and the fact that Kimberly herself does not identify as trans but sought to make a film about a trans man. Though surprised at the vehemence of the protests, which lasted 10–15 minutes before the protestors were escorted out, Kimberly stayed for another two hours to answer questions and discuss the audience's concerns.

After the success of *Boys*, producers came to Kimberly with money and ideas for new projects. At the time she read the 1994 *Village Voice* article about Brandon's murder, Kimberly had been working on a thesis film about women soldiers in the Civil War who dressed as men in order to fight. She set that project aside but never lost interest in war stories. Her 2008 film *Stop-Loss* is based on the experiences of her brother and other American soldiers who fought in Iraq. The title of the movie refers to the Bush administration's stop-loss policy that sent soldiers back to Iraq and Afghanistan on multiple tours beyond their service contracts. *Stop-Loss* depicts three soldiers who struggle with posttraumatic stress disorder but are unable to leave the war behind. Released around the time of the acclaimed film *The Hurt Locker*, directed by Kathryn Bigelow, *Stop-Loss* received mixed reviews and failed to earn back its budget.

Kimberly's next film was the 2013 remake of the Stephen King novel *Carrie*, the story of an outcast girl who wreaks her revenge against the high school classmates who tormented her. Kimberly's *Carrie* was updated to the digital age, with cyberbullying made integral to the plot. Despite mixed reviews, *Carrie* won a People's Choice award for Favorite Horror Movie in 2014.

In an interview with *Flood* magazine, Kimberly compared her experience making *Boys*, the project of her heart, to that of her two later films. She observed that, "*You* are the power of the independent movie; but once you move into the [studio] system . . . I thought my willpower was enough. But I had to learn a whole new game." With *Stop-Loss* and *Carrie*, she had to work with many other people who had their own ideas for what the movie should look like. They also had expectations for budgets, equipment, and how much the movies should earn. The "interferences against female creativity were devastating," Kimberly remarked.

Kimberly's experiences with her later films and with the obstacles that women directors face has led to her activism within the film industry. From 2016 to 2019, she headed the Director's Branch of the Academy of Motion Pictures. In this leadership role, she has sought to expand the visibility and power of women and people of color within the Academy. She noticed that many women and Black directors don't get to make movies as often as men do—a double challenge for Black women directors and one Ava DuVernay addressed after succeeding Kimberly in this leadership position—and these years-long gaps between films make it difficult for them to remain in the industry. Referring to her success with *Boys* and Kathryn Bigelow's with *The Hurt*

Locker, Kimberly asked, "Why are the women not working as much as the men, once they've had that success?" She wants to get to the bottom of this problem and find a solution that gives all women filmmakers the same chances that men have enjoyed since motion pictures began.

9

Dee Rees: Going All Out

Being able to fail and fail loudly is not celebrated enough in society. Oftentimes failure is linked to a person's character rather than considered a life event. How people respond to such a moment in their life has the potential and power to derail a person's trajectory. Dee Rees, the critically acclaimed film director, has tasted both success and failure in her career. Yet, she uses each win and loss as fuel to keep pushing the boundaries, changing the narrative, and making films more inclusive for those who identify as Black, a person of color, and/or queer.

Dee was born on February 7, 1977, in Nashville, Tennessee, into what was considered a typical middle-class family. Her father served as a local police officer, while her mother worked as a scientist at Vanderbilt University. For the most part, her childhood was fairly normal, with the exception of the neighbors who felt that her and her family didn't belong in the suburban neighborhood. There were times that she had to pick up trash that was thrown on their front yard, remove the toilet tissue off the trees, or even look at the Confederate flags that neighbors had hung in their windows. But it was those experiences that are woven into the films she directs and writes for her audiences. Most of her work can be considered semiautobiographical and deals with issues that are near and dear to her heart.

Dee left home for college in Florida and attended the historically Black Florida A&M University (FAMU), where she majored in business. As a student at FAMU, she encountered her first overt and subtle act of racism within the film industry when she went to attend a screening of *Dead Presidents*. In an interview with the *Hollywood Reporter*, she recalled, "[The theater owners] weren't selling out the theater. . . . They were saying, 'We don't want too many people in the theater at the same time. We don't want any problems at this showing.' They were actively suppressing ticket sales." This experience caused her to pay attention to how Hollywood often undervalues the work of Black artists. "That was during this blossoming of all these great Black filmmakers. . . . And even their stats got depressed."

After completing her MBA at FAMU, Dee went on to work as a branding and marketing professional. She was struggling with maintaining her work in the field and was fired from two jobs. Though it was a tough time, Dee learned a lot. "It shaped me only in that it made me very clear on what I don't want to do," she said. "Having survived a cubicle, I was super clear on why it's better to be struggling in the thing that you love to do than to be having a solidity in something that is soul-sucking."

While working on a Dr. Scholl's campaign, she fell in love with directing. The atmosphere and the crew for the commercial entranced her and fully awakened her creative side. She could not have guessed that watching an actor be placed in a specific spot to film a commercial would serve as the catalyst for her embarking upon a new career. "They were positioning the actor on a pane of glass. And putting a camera under the glass to show him jumping up and down . . . and I was like, 'I want to do this,'" Dee said. She decided to apply to New York University's graduate film production program, even though a production member told her that she would not get in the program.

Upon her acceptance, Dee quit her job and chased after her new passion—directing—a decision that convinced her parents that she had lost her mind. As she put it, "My parents thought I was having a nervous breakdown." Prior to being on set for this commercial, Dee had had no formal, or informal, television or film training. She hadn't even touched a video camera! Her business degree from Florida A&M University didn't lend itself to a career in the entertainment industry. However, her eyes had been opened to a new possibility, one that she wasn't willing to part ways with, no matter what her parents or anyone else believed.

While attending NYU, she was often overlooked and denied the assistance she needed with her assignments from her professors. It seemed as if the more gifted students received favoritism from her some of her professors. Film school was not turning out as she had envisioned. "I failed and I failed hard." For a brief moment, she thought about giving up on her new—expensive—dream. She wondered if, at 27, she could really start a new career.

Thankfully, Dee had a great support system surrounding her, including her girlfriend at the time and one of her professors, Spike Lee. He loved the way she told her stories and thought she possessed a unique rawness that wasn't common among film students—or even some seasoned directors.

Around the same time Dee was attending film school, she was also coming to terms with her sexuality and made the difficult decision to come out to her family as a lesbian. Her parents took the news hard and believed that it was a phase she was going through, like her newfound interest in filmmaking. "This double-whammy change felt like an opening up on every level, but from the outside looking in, I'm sure it looked like a midlife crisis or something," Dee said. "But it was just me getting to be myself." This was her truth—one that her parents had to come to terms with on their own. The strength she found to come out led her to create the coming-of-age film *Pariah*, which premiered in 2011 at the Sundance Film Festival. With this movie, Dee's semi-autobiographical story came to the big screen and helped create a path for others who are part of the LGBTQI+ community—especially those who are Black and feel unseen.

Support, a dream, and $50,000 are the ingredients that helped to create Dee's first feature film, *Pariah*. Following the story of 17-year-old Alike, the movie depicts a teenager who has realized she is lesbian but hasn't yet found the way to come out to her parents. Like Dee's family, Alike's family is conservative and religious. Appearances are important to maintain, even if her parent's marriage is falling apart behind closed doors. Dee is often credited for her ability as a director and writer to weave real life into each of her movies, and *Pariah* sets the precedent for this.

The movie started off as a 140-page thesis for her film class. Spike Lee encouraged her to turn the thesis into a short, offering to serve as her mentor on the film. *Pariah* soon found itself on the film circuit, and the film received several awards, opening doors for Dee in Hollywood. She would go on to direct *Bessie* for HBO and *Mudbound*, and *The Last Thing He Wanted* for Netflix. Dee could begin to tell the story of queer Black folk on a larger scale, allowing them to be seen and normalized in media. "I'm just interested in seeing myself on screen. I'm interested in seeing my community on screen. And sometimes that's not just about their identity—let them be whole characters beyond their sexuality. In that way, it normalizes it and de-otherizes who we are."

Joining the Criterion Collection

On June 29, 2021, Dee entered one of the most prestigious realms of film directors when her first featured film, *Pariah*, was added to the acclaimed Criterion Collection. As such, she is the first African American woman and first queer woman of color to receive the honor of having her film released by the organization.

The Criterion Collection started in 1984, taking classic films and bringing them to home video—or now, DVD and Blu-ray Disc. According to its website, the collection's editions of the films "include restored film transfers along with commentary tracks and other kinds of supplemental features . . . [and] each film is presented as its maker would want it seen and published in an edition that will deepen the viewer's understanding and appreciation of the art of cinema."

In 2020 the *New York Times* reported that of the 1,034 films from 450 different directors, only 4 films had Black directors. It's those types of statistics that the Criterion president, Peter Becker, acknowledged in an e-mail to the *Hollywood Reporter*, saying, there "comes a responsibility to seek out a broader and more diverse array of voices both in our library and in the curatorial community that informs our work." He continued with a promise: "We hope that the breadth of filmed expression in our disc release slate and on the Criterion Channel over the coming months and years reflects the seriousness with which we take that responsibility."

For most women and women of color in Hollywood, the ebb and flow of work can be determined by the success, critical and financial, of their last work. Dee said, "It was about convincing people that it wasn't a one-off—it wasn't a fluke," that "it wasn't the only story that I could tell." Although her latest feature for Netflix, *The Last Thing He Wanted*, received mixed reviews, it didn't stop her from getting the opportunity to direct the upcoming film adaptation of George Gershwin's opera *Porgy and Bess*. And as she was supported by Spike Lee previously, Dee has the stellar Irwin Winkler and MGM Studios backing this new venture.

Dee doesn't wait for an opportunity or for people to allow her to tell her stories. She takes what is deemed a failure and uses it as fuel for her creative energy. And Dee creates her visions as they come to her with the hope that the right one will stick.

Part III

Young Stars in a
Global Film Industry

10

Chloé Zhao: Neorealism for a New Century

In 1937 Italy's fascist dictator, Benito Mussolini, established the film studio Cinecittà in Rome to produce propaganda films and escapist entertainment for his people so they would happily march to his orders. Aware of its value to his regime—and to the Nazis who occupied Rome after a series of military defeats and a nationwide uprising deposed Mussolini in 1943—Allied forces bombed the sprawling studio complex in Rome's suburbs, destroying most of the buildings. What remained of the studio served as a refugee camp from the end of the war in 1945 until 1947.

For Italian filmmakers, the destruction of their production facility posed a major challenge to creating new work—so did the fact that they had devoted years of their lives and their considerable talents to serving a despot and his evil cause. They felt they had no choice at the time, but as the war ended and Italy was freed from fascist and Nazi forces, filmmakers sought to explore the lives of working-class people who had suffered under those regimes. For years, they had been forced to tell lies. Now they wanted to tell the truth to their country and to the world.

So began Italian neorealism, one of the most significant and influential film movements of the 20th century. In films such as Roberto Rossellini's *Rome, Open City*, which won the Palme d'Or at the 1946 Cannes Film Festival, three features characterized neorealism: The first was filming on location, in the working-class communities where stories were set, rather than in studios. The second was using nonprofessional actors from the community alongside well-known performers. The third was highlighting the harsh lives of ordinary people rather than the glamorous lives and personal intrigues of social elites. Rossellini described this new movement by saying, "I try to capture reality, nothing else."

The neorealist movement in Italy lasted until the mid-1950s, when the Cinecittà studios were rebuilt. A more prosperous and peaceful nation demanded both lighter fare and films that evoked the culture of the United States, the country that had played such a huge role in Italy's liberation and rebuilding.

Although Italian neorealism had run its course, it remained a major influence on generations of filmmakers, particularly those from communities that had experienced oppression and marginalization. In the United States after 2000, a number of women writers and directors were drawn to this genre, seeing it as a way of telling the stories of working-class people, particularly women and girls, whom society had ignored and the media had misrepresented. For the most part, the violence these women had experienced was not political but personal in the form of domestic abuse, substance abuse, poverty, and neglect.

The 2008 recession served as a watershed in recent American history. The collapse of the housing market and widespread layoffs left many people without jobs or homes. Individuals and families scraped by on temporary and part-time jobs that lacked regular hours or benefits. The journalist Jessica Bruder began to chronicle the lives of people leading this precarious, itinerant existence, fixing up vans and campers to be their shelter as they travelled from place to place working short-term, seasonal jobs in warehouses, recreational facilities, and farms. Her nonfiction book, *Nomadland: Surviving America in the Twenty-First Century*, became a bestseller when it came out in 2017.

Chloé Zhao seemed an unlikely person to turn Bruder's book into an award-winning film that would make history. She wasn't born in the United States but in Beijing, the capital of China, on March 31, 1982, with the name Zhao Ting. Her father was a high-ranking industrial manager in the Communist government, and her mother once performed in a Communist Party propaganda song and dance troupe. After her parents split up, her father married a well-known Chinese comic actor.

Chloé was a nonconformist in "an ancient culture where I was expected to be a certain way," she told John Powers at *Vogue*. She loved movies, Japanese manga, and all aspects of American popular culture. Worried for her future because of her disdain for authority, her parents sent her first to a boarding school in England and then to Mount Holyoke College in Massachusetts. She learned English but had little interest in her studies. After living in New York City for several years and working odd jobs, she applied to film school at NYU. There, she discovered her passion, and her professors discovered her talent.

Wendy and Lucy and Frozen River

In 2008, the year the Great Recession began, two films by women directors captured the lives of those left behind, even before the economy collapsed. Kelly Reichardt's *Wendy and Lucy* portrays a young woman, Wendy, on her way to Alaska with her dog, fleeing trouble and in search of a job that will allow her to support herself. When her car breaks down in a hardscrabble industrial town in Oregon and her dog, Lucy, runs away, Wendy's goal turns from her own survival to finding her dog. The film stays in the present, so the viewer has to imagine the backstory. Where is Wendy from? Is she escaping an abusive situation? How long have she and Lucy been together? Many of the townspeople are barely getting by themselves, and when they see Wendy in need, they turn away from her.

For *Wendy and Lucy*, Kelly drew inspiration from the 1952 Italian neorealist classic *Umberto D.*, directed by Vittorio De Sica, which depicts a lonely, financially struggling Italian pensioner who loses his dog after hunger ruins his health and lands him in the hospital.

Directed by Courtney Hunt, *Frozen River* is filmed on location along the border of New York State and Quebec during a long, harsh winter. Although she and Kelly were born in the same year, 1964, Courtney didn't start making films until her 40s; this release was her debut. *Frozen River* tells the story of Ray, a young mother trying to feed and house herself and her two sons after her husband has skipped town with the money they'd saved to buy a new mobile home. Many of the film's scenes take place inside the family's old, crumbling mobile home and in the dollar store that won't give Ray enough hours or promote her to a better-paying position.

Searching for her gambling-addicted husband at a casino, Ray meets a widowed Mohawk woman, Lila, who earns money by smuggling immigrants through the reservation and past the border via the iced-over river. Ray must overcome her prejudice to work with Lila, but cultures clash once again when Ray's teenage son is caught scamming an elderly Mohawk woman. Like classic neorealist films, *Frozen River* centers working-class characters and those at the margins of society.

Chloe's first film, *Songs My Brothers Taught Me*, was released in 2015. Set on the Pine Ridge Reservation in South Dakota, the movie portrays a Lakota teen coming of age amid poverty and the despair on the reservation that has led to one of the highest suicide rates in the United States. The main character, Johnny, has the opportunity to leave the reservation, but he would leave behind his mother, his younger sister, and his incarcerated older brother—siblings who have just experienced the death of their father. Like her neorealist predecessors, Chloé used non-professional actors from the reservation and scripted the film around their life stories, adjusting the plot as her young actors' circumstances changed. "The script, the story, the people and the place all exist [within each other]. It's an organic process," she told *Filmmaker* magazine in 2013 as she was filming *Songs*.

In that same interview, she talked about what drew her, as a Chinese-born filmmaker, to portray Lakota teens:

> It goes back to when I was a teenager in China, being in a place where there are lies everywhere. . . . You felt like you were never going to be able to get out. A lot of info I received when I was younger was not true, and I became very rebellious toward my family and my background. . . . Studying political science in a liberal arts college was a way for me to figure out what is

real. Arm yourself with information, and then challenge that too.

In that respect, Chloé followed the path of the Italian neo-realists who were forced to make fascist propaganda before and during World War II and were only able to tell the real stories after the war. Chloé left the land of her birth to find freedom, but when that 2013 interview was uncovered after *Nomadland*'s success, she felt the power of China's repression. In April 2021 *Time* reported that "since its initial publication, the 2013 article has been 'edited and condensed,' according to a note on *Filmmaker Magazine*'s website, with the widely quoted portion referring to Zhao's upbringing in China now omitted," so that *Nomadland* and Chloé's future films could be shown in the country. Nonetheless, *Nomadland* never opened in China, and the media there censored coverage of Chloé's awards.

Chronicles of Hardship Post-2008: Debra Granik

Before Chloé emerged as a principal filmmaker of working-class America, Debra Granik explored this territory several times in the decade following the Great Recession. Born in Cambridge, Massachusetts, in 1963, raised in the wealthy suburbs of Washington, DC, and educated at Brandeis University and NYU's film school, Debra also seemed an unlikely person to present these stories. At first, she made documentaries and docudramas about revolutionaries in Guyana (*Thunder in Guyana*), drug addiction (*Down to the Bone*), and PTSD among veterans (*Stray Dog*). Her feature films *Winter's Bone* (2010) and *Leave No Trace* (2018) connect to these projects but as fiction rather than documentary.

Based on a 2006 novel by Daniel Woodrell with the same title, *Winter's Bone* is the story of 17-year-old Ree as she tries to keep her younger siblings out of foster care after the violent death of their meth-dealing father. In order to support her family in their home, Ree must find her father's body so she can claim his life insurance, but doing so exposes her to the fury of his former associates and many of her neighbors who live off the drug trade. Filmed in the Ozarks, the film introduced the actor Jennifer Lawrence, who went on to act as Katniss Everdeen in the Hunger Games trilogy, among other notable roles. Debra also used nonprofessional actors from the area. One of those actors, Vietnam War-veteran Ron Hall, inspired both the documentary *Stray Dog* and her next feature film, *Leave No Trace*.

Leave No Trace is based on the 2009 novel *My Abandonment* by Peter Rock. It portrays a veteran of the Iraq War, Will, who has PTSD and lives in a forest encampment in western Oregon with Tom, his 13-year-old homeschooled daughter. After the authorities find Tom walking alone in the woods, the two are resettled, with Will working for a Christmas-tree farm and Tom attending a regular middle school. Will, however, is ill-suited to ordinary life, so he takes Tom back off the grid, where they join a community of people living in RVs and supporting themselves through beekeeping and subsistence agriculture—until he finds even that arrangement impossible.

Debra filmed *Leave No Trace* in part inside an RV community in Oregon and included songs performed by local folk musicians. She again introduced a previously unknown actor, the New Zealand-born Thomasin McKenzie, who went on to play a major role in 2019's surprise hit film *Jojo Rabbit*.

After *Songs My Brothers Taught Me* received notice at the major film festivals Sundance and Cannes, Chloé returned to Pine Ridge and the stories of cowboys like Johnny's father. Once again, her journey both paralleled and critiqued that of Italian filmmakers, who turned away from neorealism in the 1950s and 1960s to make "spaghetti westerns," Italian western films featuring highly stereotypical white cowboys and Native Americans, which displayed the filmmakers' admiration for American culture. Also looking in from the outside with admiration for the free spirit and resilience of the American people, Chloé challenged those stereotypes. The protagonist of her 2017 film, *The Rider*, Brady Blackburn, is not white and not a figure from the long-gone past but an enrolled member of the Lower Brulé Lakota today, as is the actor who played him, Brady Jandreau.

The Rider is based on Jandreau's experience of suffering a near-fatal head injury during a bronco-riding competition and learning he can no longer compete. Brady, the character, is torn between his doctor's orders and his desire to ride and tame seemingly untamable horses. In a glowing review in *Vogue*, John Powers wrote, "What drives Zhao's film forward is a question of identity: If he can't ride—if he's been stripped of the work that provides a sense of purpose and dignity to his life—who is he? *The Rider* isn't merely about cowboys or the West, but about manhood in America."

In contrast to Chloé's two earlier films drawn from the lives of her actors, *Nomadland* began with a script, which she adapted from Bruder's book. The original idea for the film came from Frances McDormand, the veteran actor who had already won an Academy Award for her performance in the 1996 detective thriller *Fargo*. She and producer Peter Spears had optioned the book and offered to fund Chloé's work on *Nomadland* because of their admiration for *Songs* and *The Rider*. Frances played the leading role of Fern, who takes to the road in a battered van after her husband dies and the factory that supported them and their rural Nevada community shuts down. Supporting her travels (barely) through short-term jobs at an Amazon warehouse and a campsite, Fern meets other middle-aged and elderly nomads and is tempted to settle down when she falls in love with a veteran, Dave, who has recently become a grandfather.

Among the nonprofessional actors who appear in *Nomadland* is Bob Wells, the organizer of an annual meetup in Arizona that Fern attends over the one-and-a-half-year time span of the film. Chloé filmed *Nomadland* over the course of five months, though she and her crew had to return to one place in South Dakota several months later because a snowstorm interrupted their work.

In a panel coinciding with *Nomadland*'s wide theatrical release in 2021, Chloé talked about the process of filming within marginalized communities and gaining the trust of the people. Because the filmmakers were mostly from New York City and Los Angeles and at least a generation younger than their subjects, it was important to have crew members be sensitive and "listen well." She also talked about the challenges of choosing among the dozens of stories in Bruder's book to focus on "a simple, relatable emotional arc for one character."

Neorealism and the Abortion Debate: *Never Rarely Sometimes Always*

The winner of the 2020 Sundance Film Festival's Special Jury Award for Neo-Realism was Eliza Hittman's *Never Rarely Sometimes Always*. The film portrays a pregnant working-class teenager from a small town in Pennsylvania who cannot get an abortion where she lives. Accompanied by her cousin, she takes a bus to New York City. The girls are trapped there for several days with little money and no place to stay, because the pregnancy crisis center in her town misjudged the time she has been pregnant and the procedure is more complicated. Eliza filmed in a Planned Parenthood facility, and the teenagers who played the main characters were from the same town in upstate New York, in their first professional acting roles. Though Eliza wrote the screenplay, the film has the feel of a documentary because of the new and nonprofessional actors, the on-location filming in New York City, and its willingness to take on a controversial yet relatable topic with sensitivity and nuance through the eyes of its frightened young protagonist.

Two women were nominated in 2021 for the Academy Award for Best Director for the first time ever—the other, Emerald Fennell, for her revenge thriller *Promising Young Woman*. When Chloé won, she became only the second woman (after Kathryn Bigelow) to take that Oscar and the first woman of color to do so. In addition, she took home an Oscar for Best Adapted Screenplay, Frances won for Best Actress, and *Nomadland* won Best Picture. Chloé was also the second woman (after Barbra Streisand) and first woman of color to win a Golden Globe for Best Director, and the film won for Best Picture in the drama category.

The original neorealist movement in Italy lasted approximately ten years, but its impact has reverberated for many decades and will continue to do so as long as there are economic, social, and political struggles and filmmakers willing and able to show the truth. For Chloé, it is time for a new direction. She is now directing films in the Marvel franchise, with the release of *Eternals* in fall 2021. Despite the constraints of working within a popular franchise, Chloé has found ways to give the film her own stamp using "practical locations," as opposed to studio sets and computer-generated effects, as Marvel Studios president Kevin Feige explained to *Variety*. And for Chloé, who grew up reading comics to the consternation of her parents and teachers in China, making films for Marvel has meant a return to her roots—while still telling stories in her own way.

Patty Jenkins's Journey to the DC Universe

Chloé's journey from directing small realistic films to blockbusters in the Marvel universe follows in the footsteps of other acclaimed women directors. The best known is Patty Jenkins, who debuted in 2003 with the crime drama *Monster*. Based on the true story of Aileen Wuornos, a serial killer executed in Florida, the film explores what drove her to kill seven men and her girl-friend's growing suspicions of her. Charlize Theron won an Academy Award for Best Actress and a Golden Globe for her role as Wuornos, and the American Film Institute chose *Monster* as Movie of the Year.

After *Monster*, Patty directed commercials and TV pilots and episodes, winning several Emmy nominations over the following decade. Her commercial break occurred when she was hired to direct the first *Wonder Woman*, released in 2017. *Wonder Woman* became one of that year's top-grossing movies, and Patty became a go-to director for big-budget films from popular franchises.

In 2020 the sequel *Wonder Woman 1984* was released amid the COVID-19 pandemic. Most movie theaters were closed to prevent the spread of the deadly virus, so *WW84* premiered on the streaming service HBO Max. Home viewing on the small screen proved a challenge for a film meant to be shown in public, on a large screen, and with a powerful sound system. The movie received poor reviews. Its worldwide gross, about $166 million by mid-2021, was a fraction of the more than $800 million that *Wonder Woman* had brought in. Despite this hiccup, Patty has continued to dominate big-budget films. She is set to direct *Wonder Woman 3* and, in a new franchise for her, the Star Wars movie *Rogue Squadron*.

Born in 1971 the daughter of an air force pilot, Patty found inspiration in comics and the *Superman* movie. She studied painting as an undergraduate at Cooper Union in New York City and received her MFA in directing at the American Film Institute. After her success with *Monster*, she saw that indie filmmaking lacked the opportunities of "tentpoles"—big-budget productions of established franchises that support a studio's overall health. Making TV pilots taught her how to handle large budgets. As she told Cara Buckley of the *New York Times*, "The TV projects I was doing were getting to $11 million or $12 million, shooting over an eight-to-10-day period, shutting down the Chicago River with helicopters and 1,000 people."

This big-budget power has allowed Patty to demand more from the film industry and to make history in doing so. As a condition for making *WW84*, she insisted on equal pay for herself and her female colleagues. Ultimately, she was paid $9 million for the film. With *Rogue Squadron*, Patty has again broken new ground as the first woman to direct a Star Wars movie.

Petra Costa: Documenting the Personal and the Political

At the beginning of 1990, when Petra Costa was about to turn seven, her older sister, Elena, announced that she would be leaving their home in Belo Horizonte, Brazil, to become an actor in New York City. Petra had always been close to her sister. Elena, who was 13 years older than Petra, was like another mother to her, especially after their parents divorced before Petra's second birthday.

Elena had always wanted to be an actor, following in the footsteps of their mother, Marília "Li An" Andrade, who had briefly acted in her teens before joining a leftist political group in the 1960s, around the time of a coup that ushered in two decades of military dictatorship in Brazil. Li An's and her boyfriend's political affiliations forced them to go underground. Because she was pregnant with Elena at the time, Li An couldn't take part in the kind of guerrilla campaigns that over the next few years would lead to the deaths of many of their friends. Elena was raised in hiding, prohibited from talking about her family. Going outside the home meant putting on an act. Elena became very good at it, and she eventually was passionate about making it her career.

Born on July 8, 1983, Petra grew up after democracy came to Brazil and her parents had come out of hiding. Still, she absorbed Elena's passion for the theater as Elena directed Petra, their mother, and their nanny in home movies that Elena scripted. Although Elena had attracted attention in Brazil for her dramatically choreographed stage performances, she had limited prospects if she wanted to pursue film rather than theater. Brazil's film industry was less developed in the late 1980s, and actresses typically played stereotypical roles in a sexist culture. In New York City, she videorecorded her impressions of daily life, but after several months, she had become despondent, unable to find work despite her talent, her poise, and her fluency in multiple languages. She developed an eating disorder, and when she returned to Brazil for a visit, her mother decided to move into an apartment with her in New York and bring seven-year-old Petra as well.

Petra started school in New York, learned English, and made friends despite her troubled home life. With no prospects for acting work, Elena's mental state deteriorated, and in November 1990, she took her life. Petra and her mother left New York shortly afterward. Li An told Petra she didn't want her to become an actor, or to live in New York.

Petra would defy both those wishes. At the age of 14, she began acting as well. Several years later, she joined a theater workshop that assigned the creation of a "book of life," an autobiography in dramatic form. Petra searched for her diaries, and along with them, she found Elena's diaries and video recordings. Petra was stunned by the similarities between her reflections and those of a sister who she'd known for less than half her life.

Like her sister, Petra studied theater at the University of São Paulo, but unlike her sister, she wanted to study the broader social context underlying theater, literature, and film. She applied to Barnard College, a partner of Columbia University in New York City, and moved there in 2003, when she was 20 years old—the same age Elena was when she first went there. In this second journey, Petra thrived. As she told an interviewer from the alumni magazine,

> The moment I arrived in New York, the phantoms of my sister quickly dissolved. . . . I quickly started to make my own path and really fell in love with the whole atmosphere, just being in such a rich environment, exchanging so many ideas, and being challenged intellectually in so many ways. I felt clearly that I found my identity.

Petra graduated with highest honors, majoring in anthropology. After briefly working for a television company, she moved to London to study public health at the London School of Economics, specializing in the experience of trauma. She received her master's degree in 2008 and returned to Brazil. It seemed that she'd moved on from her interest in acting, but while home for vacations and after graduation, she videorecorded interviews with her grandparents. In 2009 she turned these recordings of their lives into a short film, *Undertow Eyes*, a meditation on their enduring love as they grew older and contemplated death. The home movies Petra and her sister used to make inspired this effort, along with her future documentaries that drew on her family's history.

Undertow Eyes attracted the attention of major filmmakers both in and outside Brazil, including Fernando Meirelles and Tim Robbins. Through them, Petra secured the funding to make her first full-length film—*Elena*, the story of her sister's life and tragic death.

Described by the Brazilian entertainment magazine *Guia da Semana* as "a balance of documentary and poetry," *Elena* draws on home movies, diary entries, interviews with some 50 people who knew her, and other sources. Along with these artifacts are recreations of events in which Petra and her mother perform in a choreography in which it is sometimes difficult to tell what is past and what is present, what is true and what is imagined, and whether the person the viewer sees is Elena,

Petra, or their mother. In order to create that last effect, Petra dyed her hair a darker shade, closer to the color of her sister's and mother's. The poetic voice-over, set amid images of women in loose, translucent dresses swimming underwater (an evocation of Shakespeare's character Ophelia in *Hamlet*), describes her sister as "my inconsolable memory made of shadow and stone." When asked about whether *Elena* reopened old family wounds, Petra told Brazil's *AdoroCinema*,

> It was a mixture of joy and pain. The joyful part was that I gained a sister through this process since I had so few memories of Elena, as I was so young and saw her as something of a legend. Through the film, I came to see her as a human being, flesh and bone, in all her dimensions. But it was like I was constantly gaining a sister and then losing her again, since she was no longer with us. At the same time, the pain was greater because I was better able to understand what really happened and how tragic it was.

Surrealistic Influences: Agnès Varda

Elena infuses the realistic form of the documentary with surrealistic elements. Petra cites the pioneering French director Agnès Varda as one of her principal influences. Born in Belgium in 1928, Agnès is considered the grandmother of French New Wave cinema and a pioneering feminist director. She made many short and full-length documentaries as well as fiction films. Using French New Wave techniques shared by Italian neorealism, Agnès shot these films on location and used nonprofessional actors. Before making films, she worked as an art photographer, and her films make use of still photos, poetic imagery, and nonlinear storytelling that blurs the line between past and present, and dream and reality.

Agnès mined her personal history for many of her documentaries. Her 1991 film *Jacquot de Nantes* is a tribute to the life of her husband, Jacques Demy, who died the previous year. *The Beaches of Agnès*, released in 2008, is an autobiographical essay that shows a large photo of the filmmaker surrounded by smaller photos of the male directors who were part of French New Wave. Other documentaries explored political topics, among them the 1968 short film *Black Panthers*, which featured the organization's cofounder Huey P. Newton. Agnès continued to release new films up to her death at the age of 90 in 2019.

Released to near-universal critical acclaim in 2012, *Elena* attracted an unusually large audience for a documentary in

Brazil, with over 50,000 viewers in its first months. It raised awareness of suicide, a taboo topic in Brazil, and Petra spoke to the media and school and community groups about mental health and suicide prevention, where her graduate studies contributed to her expertise.

In Petra's next film, the 2015 documentary *Olmo and the Seagull*, she collaborated with the Danish filmmaker Lea Glob through a program that connected directors from South America and Africa with ones from Europe. Petra returned to some of the themes and storytelling techniques she explored in *Elena*. *Olmo* is the story of a young actor, Olivia Corsini, and her boyfriend, Serge Nicolai, who hope to star in an adaptation of Anton Chekhov's *The Seagull*. At the beginning of rehearsals, Olivia finds out she's pregnant, and when the pregnancy becomes complicated, she has to make difficult choices for herself, her career, and her unborn child. With echoes of Chekhov's classic play, *Olmo* explores success and failure, love and sacrifice, and the blurred boundaries of fiction and reality.

Family Secrets in Film: Sarah Polley

Best known as an actor since she was a small child, Sarah Polley is also the director of the highly-regarded films *Away from Her* (2006) and *Take This Waltz* (2011) as well as the documentary of her theatrical family's history and secrets, *Stories We Tell* (2012). Born in 1979 in Toronto, she is the daughter of the well-known stage, TV, and film per-formers Michael and Diane Polley. Until her mother's death from cancer when Sarah was 11, she acted alongside her parents, though Michael cut back to support his family as an insurance agent. Sarah's success as a child actor allowed her to move from home and live independently, though somewhat precariously, when she was 15.

Until 2010 Sarah acted in many of Canada's signature films and TV series. As she moved into directing, she investi-gated her family's history and the impact of celebrity on her parents, her four siblings, and herself. In research-ing her parents' past, she discovered that Michael was not her biological father. Her mother had an affair with a producer while working on a film in Montreal, which had resulted in her mother's pregnancy with Sarah.

From her teenage years on, Sarah has been an outspoken political activist in Canada on issues such as women's rights, militarism, the environment, corporate power, and poverty and income inequality. In 1991 the 12-year-old actor angered Disney executives by wearing a peace sign to a major film industry event to protest the Gulf War. Five years later, Sarah gave an interview to a teen talk show where she denounced most celebrities for choos-ing noncontroversial forms of activism rather than "really challenging the system that creates this growing disparity between the rich and the poor." In 2017 Sarah coura-geously spoke out again as one of the first women in the film industry who revealed her own mistreatment at the hands of producer Harvey Weinstein.

In her first documentaries, Petra explored personal topics that became political. For instance, *Elena* opened up conversations in Brazil about generational trauma—traumatic events experienced by previous generations that affect the lives of children—and the realities of depression and suicide. However, in her next film, *The Edge of Democracy*, which released in 2019, she investigated a political topic through a complicated personal lens.

In 2014 while Petra was working on *Olmo*, Brazil held a hard-fought election between the incumbent, Dilma Rousseff, the country's first woman president, and Aécio Neves, a conservative senator from a prominent political family. When Aécio lost, he refused to concede and encouraged a campaign in the legislature to reverse the election by impeaching Dilma. The Car Wash bribery scandal involving business leaders and politicians of all major political parties (though excluding Dilma herself) added fuel to the fire.

Petra had family members on all sides as well, and she used this to complicate and facilitate her exploration of the political turmoil in *The Edge of Democracy*. Her mother was a close friend of Dilma Rousseff's popular predecessor, the left-wing leader Luiz Inácio Lula da Silva, known worldwide as Lula. After renouncing his revolutionary past, Petra's father, Manoel Costa, had worked for Aécio Neves. Members of Manoel's family had connections with the military that had ruled Brazil for 21 years. Petra's grandfather on her mother's side cofounded the second largest construction company in Brazil, Andrade Gutierrez. That company, as Petra pointed out in the film, was involved with the Car Wash scandal. After Dilma's impeachment, a conservative prosecutor, overstepping his authority, had Lula arrested and removed from the ticket in the 2018 presidential election. This paved the way for the victory of the authoritarian populist and former military officer Jair Bolsonaro, known as "Trump of the Tropics."

In the course of filming the documentary spanning Dilma Rousseff's impeachment, Lula's arrest, and Jair Bolsonaro's victory—2016 to 2018—Petra's family connections gave her access to all of the political figures involved. Interspersed with these interviews are news footage, photos and movies of Petra's family, and stunning scenes of the presidential palace and other buildings in Brasília, the utopian capital city designed by Brazilian architect Oscar Niemeyer. Like *Elena* and *Olmo*, *Edge* is visually a work of art, with shots of a giant esplanade where red-shirted supporters of Lula and Dilma Rousseff face off against yellow-shirted Jair Bolsonaro supporters, with police and fences keeping them apart. Petra's poetic voice-over talks of a country coming apart, in the process of losing a democracy that Petra believed, as she told progressive broadcaster Michael Brooks, "was my birthright, achieved from a lifetime of my parents' struggle."

In a Q and A for the showing of *Edge* at the Museum of Modern Art in New York City, Petra spoke about the personal side of what it is like to live in a country sliding into authoritarianism, connecting it to the situation in the United States:

> It became a trauma in so many people's lives to understand that the idea of democracy from which you have a certainty that somehow you can decide on who is your president and who will represent you is completely demolished. And you understand that that certainty was an illusion, that your vote can be ripped apart. . . . It was traumatic to me in a physical way.

The Documentary Filmmaker and the Scoop: Laura Poitras

One of the publications that has investigated corruption in Brazil, the rise of the far right, and the collusion of politicians and judges in prosecuting Lula is the *Intercept*, cofounded by (among others) journalists Glenn Greenwald and Laura Poitras. Born in Boston in 1964, Laura gained fame through her reporting of national security disclosures, including those of Edward Snowden, Julian Assange, and Reality Winner.

Laura's first documentary, *Flag Wars*, about the impact of gentrification in Columbus, Ohio, was shown as part of the PBS series *POV* in 2003. Her next film, the 2006 documentary *My Country, My Country*, portrayed life for Iraqi civilians under US occupation and marked the start of her work on exposing the brutality of US foreign policy. *The Oath*, released in 2010, depicted two Yemeni men accused of terrorism.

Laura gained worldwide attention in 2014 with the release of *Citizenfour*. The year before, she had been one of the journalists to interview Edward Snowden, when he fled to Hong Kong, about his defection with classified documents and his reasons for his actions. In 2015 *Citizenfour* won the Academy Award for Best Documentary Feature.

When it was shown on Netflix in the United States, *Edge* received positive reviews and an Academy Award nomination for Best Documentary Feature. A. O. Scott of the *New York Times* called it "searing and enlightening . . . a chronicle of civic betrayal and the abuse of power, and also of heartbreak." He praised Petra's "candor" in expressing her sympathies with the side of Lula and Dilma (and her mother), writing that it "enhances rather than undermines the credibility of her report." Reviewers in Brazil were not so generous. Opinions coalesced along ideological lines, and right-wing journalists rushed to uncover scandalous details about Petra and her family. Supporters of Jair Bolsonaro flooded online sites worldwide with one-star reviews for the film, counterbalancing the reviews of her supporters and film critics outside Brazil. These efforts—often anonymous, usually cruel, and far more impactful because of social media—seemed to prove Petra's point about the dangers of political polarization and right-wing populism.

In contrast to her earlier documentaries, *Edge* appears in both Portuguese and English versions. It is not only a political history of Brazil and a personal history of a Brazilian family but also a cautionary tale for the United States—a country where Petra received so much of her education—and for the world. Petra begins her narrative in *Edge* with the words "Brazilian democracy and I are almost the same age. And I thought that in our thirties we would both be standing on solid ground." Yet, as was pointed out in many of her appearances in the US, not even a democracy of 240 years is necessarily standing on solid ground. At least in her films, Petra has constructed universal stories of who we are and our responsibilities to each other on a solid foundation of personal history and lived experience.

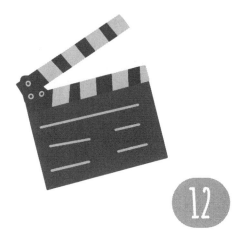

Mindy Kaling: The Power of Other

She walks into the room; everyone's attention is focused on her as she takes a seat at the table. It's her first day on the job, and she's nervous about whether her jokes will land the same way she rehearsed in her head. Mindy Kaling isn't sure how this day will go, but at 24 years old, she has landed a dream job as a new writer for NBC's breakout show *The Office*. At this time, Mindy is both the only woman and the only person of color on the writing team of nine for the show's inaugural season.

Before she was a writer, producer, director, and actor on *The Office*—where she played Kelly Kapoor—she grew up in Cambridge, Massachusetts. Born in the summer of 1979, Mindy, whose full name is Vera Mindy Chokalingam, and her older brother were raised by their father, a Tamil architect, and mother, a Bengali ob-gyn. Her parents met each other in Lagos, Nigeria, and then immigrated to the United States the same year Mindy was born. From an early age, Mindy had a knack for comedy and loved making others laugh. She and her friend Mavis "bonded over comedy." As she shares in her best-selling book of personal essays, *Is Everyone Hanging Out Without Me? (And Other Concerns)*, "It didn't matter if it was good or bad; at fourteen, we didn't really know the difference. We were comedy nerds, and we just loved watching and talking about it nonstop." The pair would get together on Saturdays to watch "*Dr. Katz, Kids in the Hall,* or *Saturday Night Live* reruns, but when those were over, we were lucky if there was some dated movie playing like *Porky's* or *Kentucky Fried Movie.*"

But she didn't start testing out her writing chops until she began her undergraduate studies at Dartmouth, where she graduated with a degree in playwriting. In fact, her college experience was a marked improvement from her high school days: "I was freakin' jaws in a community swimming pool. I wrote plays, I acted, I sang, I was the student newspaper cartoonist."

However, she still had a lot to learn. One of her biggest dreams at the time was to be a writer for *Late Night with Conan O'Brien*. Really she just wanted to be close to the person she deemed to be the coolest human on the planet. She managed to secure an internship for the show. As she fondly remembers, she "was famously one of the worst interns the program had ever seen. The reason I was bad was because I treated my internship as a free ticket to watch my hero perform live on stage every day, and not as a way to help the show run smoothly by doing errands."

This would have derailed most people from moving forward with their aspirations. But Mindy persevered and stayed the course of pursuing her dreams to break into the industry. After she graduated from college, she and two of her best friends moved to Brooklyn, Mindy hoping to strike it big. Not having any money to take screenwriting courses, she spent time at the Lincoln Center Barnes and Noble's film and television section. "I spent hours sitting in the aisle, copying down sections in a loose-leaf notebook," she recalled. Within all those hours she learned what she needed to get her foot in the door: a sample script, also called a "spec." "That's when I started working on my first spec, a Will and Grace sample, having seen the show only a handful of times." When she finished writing it, she sent it over to NBC. The station declined to even look at her spec.

Undeterred, Mindy enlisted the help of her best friend, Brenda Withers, to write a play. Together, the two young women created a play called *Matt and Ben*, which was their funny take on how Matt Damon and Ben Affleck became inspired to write the movie *Good Will Hunting*.

The Birth of Matt and Ben

Matt and Ben was a way for both Mindy and Brenda to get their creative juices flowing. While living in New York to pursue her dream of becoming an actor or writer, Mindy was starting to believe she was destined to become nothing more than a glorified babysitter. "Because no one was hiring us to act or write, Brenda and I decided to create something to perform in ourselves." The play spawned from the two best friends goofing off, discussing Harry Potter and watching the latest episodes of Judge Judy. Mindy and Brenda, being up to date on pop culture, often joked about Matt and Ben. But eventually the pair started taking the bits from these charades to create characters.

At the time, Ben Affleck and Matt Damon were huge Hollywood stars who happened to be childhood best friends. Together they had written a movie script, which became the critically praised *Good Will Hunting*. The women decided to not focus on when the men became famous, Oscar-winning actors but rather to imagine what life was like for them before the lights, camera, and action. "We did no research on the actual people, because we didn't care about their actual pasts; the real Matt Damon and Ben Affleck were simply jumping-off points for our Matt and Ben."

To save money for putting the production together, Mindy and Brenda enlisted the help of their other best friend—Jocelyn—and another friend to help produce the play. And, of course, both Mindy and Brenda starred in and directed the play. For wardrobe the pair borrowed Brenda's brother's clothes. They were playing guys, after all, and needed to dress the part. And then the impossible happened: the play grew legs of its own and took off! They entered the play in the New York International Fringe Festival and the play was named Best Overall Production in 2002, beating out 500 other plays. Soon producers came knocking, and the play received an actual budget, a new director, and even a wardrobe—allowing them to return Brenda's brother's clothes.

Mindy's play with her best friend did so well that it was invited to the US Comedy Arts Festival in Aspen, Colorado. The huge comedy show was sponsored by HBO and offered the opportunity the for the duo to get more eyes on their show. Except, the folks in Aspen were not impressed with the play at all. It didn't help that *Matt and Ben* was the only play in the festival that usually showcased stand-up comedy acts and that the play itself was an hour long whereas the other acts were 30 minutes at most. The attendees in Colorado were not interested in anything the ladies had to offer. "We'd hear the door open, light would stream in, and then we'd hear the conversation the leavers would have with the people waiting in line for the act scheduled to follow us." And the comments were not favorable.

Although the play bombed at the festival, with the help of Mindy's agent, they were able to get a now-defunct network to pick it up for pilot season. Unfortunately, the pilot season became a nonstarter for them. One reason was that the two women would not star in the show. Instead, the new potential show—*Mindy and Brenda*—would feature two other actors who didn't resemble the pair. The other reason was that the script was changed to the point that it was unrecognizable to Mindy and Brenda. The pilot was an epic flop, which would later prove to be a blessing in disguise for Mindy. While her agent was disappointed, Mindy was relieved that her name would not be attached to the show in any capacity, thus allowing her to embrace a fresh opportunity for new show called *The Office.*

Before Mindy had the opportunity to start directing and producing episodes of *The Office*, she had to overcome her anxiety and imposter syndrome in her role as a staff writer. Of course, she was funny, but she was in a space with writers who had years of experience writing for comedy shows. "Joking around with Brenda and writing plays on the floor of our living room in Brooklyn was intimate and safe, and entwined in our friendship. But I wasn't friends with these guys."

A Day at *The Office*

As noted earlier, *Matt and Ben* was a huge hit in New York. It eventually ran off-Broadway at the historic PS (public school) 112. During one of these showings, Greg

Daniels and his wife, Susan, were in the audience. Greg had created the British version of *The Office*, which NBC had picked up mid-season for the US market and given the green light for six episodes. After the show, Mindy received a call from her agent saying that Greg wanted to have a general meeting, or "general," with her. As Mindy prepared for the meeting, she became nervous realizing all the work Greg had done, including the creation of the TV show *King of the Hill*. "Most of the time with generals, neither person knows exactly why they are meeting the other person. . . . The meetings are fun if you like chatting, which I do, but frustrating if you like moving forward with your life, which I also do. But usually, you get a free bottle of water," Mindy describes in her book.

Her meeting with Greg proved to be no different, as it was filled with long and awkward pauses. Mindy left the meeting not knowing what would happen next. She continued to look for other writing opportunities with various television networks, but nothing was panning out. Thankfully, she didn't have to wait too long before fate knocked at her door, and within a week, she received a call from her agent informing her that Greg wanted to hire her as a staff writer for six episodes of *The Office*. "This was the smallest amount of contracted work you could do and

> still qualify for Writers Guild membership. I didn't care. I was a television writer! With health insurance!"

Over time she found her voice and groove with the guys. The job didn't feel as daunting, and it actually became something she looked forward to doing. Mindy stayed with the show until 2012, when her contract was up with NBC. She set her sights on creating her own show and wanted to do other creative projects. Her namesake show, *The Mindy Project*, is described as the "sitcom equivalent of a '90s rom-com brought up-to-date and up-to-the-minute, packed with pop-culture references and a knowing irony." The show follows an over-the-top ob-gyn, Dr. Mindy Lahiri (played by Mindy herself), and her quest to find love.

Currently, Mindy is still writing, directing, and producing. Her latest project, *The Sex Lives of College Girls*, is playing on HBO Max. The show follows a set of four women as they navigate their freshman year. And while she enjoys writing new projects and acting, she still had another thing to check off her list: becoming a mother. "I [didn't] want to wake up and just never be able to, because more than writing and creating shows, my great dream in life was to become a mom, because of my relationship with my mom." In 2017 Mindy gave birth to her daughter, and in 2020, she had a son— showing that dreams really do come true.

Lulu Wang: Portraying Immigrants Between Two Worlds

Since 1995 the radio show–podcast *This American Life* has entertained and informed listeners with personal stories of people famous and unknown speaking on timely, poignant, or unusual themes. One of 2016's themes was "In Defense of Ignorance," which explored how not knowing the truth can bring happiness.

Chinese American filmmaker Lulu Wang contributed the first story, "What You Don't Know," on this theme. She spoke about her 80-year-old paternal grandmother's diagnosis with advanced lung cancer and the family's decision to keep it a secret from this sturdy matriarch who'd fought alongside the Communist rebels as a teenager. Lulu's Nai Nai (grandmother) lived in Changchun, Jilin, China, in the same apartment building as her younger sister, who Lulu called Little Nai Nai. Little

Nai Nai spearheaded the campaign to keep the illness a secret because she believed it would prolong Nai Nai's life.

The lie required elaborate ruses: A medical report was faked. A cousin hastily scheduled their wedding celebration, so the entire family could gather in China with Nai Nai one last time. The attendees pretended this was a happy time when it was in fact a goodbye—in a culture where emotional expressions are strictly prescribed. They told Nai Nai that everyone was crying "tears of joy."

As Lulu prepared to leave China, she learned that Nai Nai had concealed not only her late husband's liver cancer from him but also her own bout with breast cancer from the rest of the family nine years earlier. Lulu's mother revealed that she, like Lulu, doubted the plan to lie but went along with it for the sake of the family. "That's China. That's a different world," she told Lulu. Although doctors believed she had three months to live, at the time of the broadcast—three years later—Nai Nai was still alive.

Born February 25, 1983, in Beijing, the capital of China, Lulu grew up between two worlds. Her father was a Chinese diplomat in the Soviet Union during the final decade of the Cold War, and her mother worked as a culture critic for Beijing's *Literary Gazette*. In her early years, Lulu spent time in Changchun, where her grandparents and other relatives cared for her. When Communist regimes in the Soviet Union and Eastern Europe began to collapse, Lulu's father decided to leave

China and get a PhD at the University of Miami. Lulu came to the United States with her parents when she was six, and her younger brother was born in Miami shortly afterward. Despite knowing multiple languages and working in an important position, Lulu's father at first could not get work that matched his skills, and he delivered pizzas to support his family.

Capturing the Jewish Immigrant Experience: Joan Micklin Silver

The experience of immigrants taking menial jobs after having worked in prestigious positions in their old country is a common one, as is their struggle to adapt to different values and ways of life. Before Lulu portrayed a Chinese family struggling to reconcile two cultures, the 20th-century director Joan Micklin Silver made films that portrayed the lives of Jewish immigrants in New York City.

Joan Micklin was born in Omaha, Nebraska, in 1935, the daughter of Russian Jewish immigrants who moved to the Midwest in search of better opportunities. Her father founded a successful lumber business. In 1967 Joan moved to New York City with her husband, a real estate developer, and began writing educational programs for children while raising three children of her own. With her first film, *Hester Street*, she adapted a short story by the acclaimed immigrant writer Abraham Cahan. Her husband financed the low-budget production, which featured dialogue in Yiddish.

Released in 1975, *Hester Street* portrays an immigrant, Yankel, whose wife and son have reunited with him in New York after three years of separation. Yankel, however, has become Americanized, changing his name to Jake, shaving off his beard, and falling in love with another woman. The film contains both serious and comedic elements as Jake tries to keep parts of his life secret and everyone encounters the difficulties and misunderstandings of a new language and culture. Critics praised the film, which netted a profit for the Silverses' production company and an Oscar nomination for Carol Kane, who played Yankel's wife.

Joan's best-known film was her 1988 release, *Crossing Delancey*, a romantic comedy that explores the lives of the next generation, those with immigrant grandparents. Like *Hester Street*, it involves a love triangle, with Isabelle, an aspiring writer raised in a traditional Jewish family, torn between a big-name author and the working-class boy her Bubbe (grandmother) wants her to marry.

Joan directed a dozen other films for theaters and television over a career that spanned almost thirty years, and she inspired other screenwriters and directors to portray immigration stories drawn from their backgrounds. She died in December 2020 at the age of 85.

Lulu attended Boston College and majored in literature and music. In her senior year, she took two film courses and made several short films; in 2007, two years after graduating, Lulu moved to Los Angeles. She interned for a producer, learning to coordinate the business aspects of making a film, and became friends with the Swiss aspiring-filmmaker Bernadette Bürgi. Lulu and Bernadette founded Flying Box Productions, which produced the 2014 film *Posthumous*, Lulu's feature-film debut as a director and screenwriter.

Set in Berlin, *Posthumous* represents a collaboration of actors and production teams from the United States and Germany. The film is a romantic comedy involving an American sculptor, Liam, who hasn't achieved the success he'd hoped for. A series of misadventures in the German capital ends up with a dead man in possession of Liam's identification, and now the world believes Liam is dead. Suddenly there's interest in his work. Liam pretends to be his brother and falls in love with the American journalist sent to cover the presumably dead artist's career.

The film makes light of many artists' belief that they will be more famous in death than in life. While reviews were mixed and the film found a larger audience outside the US—it opened in Zurich, Switzerland, Bernadette's home country—critics judged Lulu as a director to watch. On the review site *Consequence* (formerly *Consequence of Sound*), Sarah Kurchak wrote, "*Posthumous* still manages to charm more often than it disappoints. And it firmly establishes Lulu Wang as an artist who won't have to wait until after her death to be appreciated in her field."

The film had already given Lulu visibility and credibility as a director when she appeared on *This American Life* and shared her story of taking part in the wedding that was also supposed to be a goodbye to her grandmother. She had wanted to make a feature film about this experience, and luckily the program captured the attention of producers. Chris Weitz, who wrote and directed the highly successful film *About a Boy*, heard the broadcast and agreed to finance the film. Even Lulu was shocked at his eagerness to commit to the project, as she told reporters:

> When I was first pitching it, it's almost like you want to start by saying, "I know this sounds crazy, but I want to make an American film—meaning tonally American, American financed—that's like 100% Asian or American-Asian cast and 75% in Mandarin with subtitles. Cool, right? Green light? Where's the money?"

The Sundance Institute, a premier incubator of independent films in North America, chose Lulu as a mentee in its 2017 FilmTwo Initiative, which works with filmmakers who have already released one feature film and are seeking to break out with their second. After polishing her script, Lulu sought out actors fluent in Mandarin Chinese who could bridge the gap between American and Chinese culture. Her search brought her to the New York–born actor, rapper, and television host Awkwafina for the leading role.

Versatile Asian-American Performer: Awkwafina

Awkwafina was born Nora Lum on June 2, 1988, the daughter of a Chinese American father and a Korean American mother. She grew up in Queens, raised by her paternal grandparents after her mother's death. They owned one of the oldest Chinese restaurants in the heavily Asian American neighborhood of Flushing. Showing early talent in music, Awkwafina graduated from a New York City public school that specialized in performing arts and received her bachelor's degree in women's studies and journalism from the University at Albany. She worked in publishing while trying to establish herself as a rapper, using the name Awkwafina, which she'd created in high school by playing off PepsiCo's bottled-water brand Aquafina.

Awkwafina's first rap video went viral in 2012 but cost her a publishing job when her employers became aware of its sexually suggestive content. Undeterred by this setback, she continued to make music and released the album *Yellow Ranger* in 2014 while working as a DJ. In 2016 she and three other Asian American rappers were featured in the documentary *Bad Rap*, which explores the challenges Asian American performers face in the genre. That year, she also made her feature-film acting debut in the comedy *Neighbors 2: Sorority Rising*.

Besides acting in significant roles in *Crazy Rich Asians*, *Ocean's Eight*, and *The Farewell*, Awkwafina did voice work for TV shows for children and adults. In 2020 she launched a regular series for Comedy Central, *Awkwafina Is Nora from Queens*, a loosely autobiographical, R-rated take on her young adult years.

Despite playing a small part in her first feature film in 2016, Awkwafina attracted the attention of the prominent Asian American comedian Margaret Cho and TV and film directors. This led Awkwafina to larger roles in the hit 2018 films *Crazy Rich Asians* and *Ocean's Eight*. When she heard about the script for *The Farewell* and its focus on main character Billi's relationship with her grandmother, she begged to audition for Lulu's film.

At first Lulu was skeptical. After all, Awkwafina was known for raunchy rather than dignified, multilayered comedy. But the audition tape made Lulu realize, as she told *Rolling Stone*, "how wonderfully raw she was, how she just sort of oozed Queens." Lulu continued, "It was like 'Oh, she could be the black sheep of this family.' . . . She wasn't going to fit in with everybody else. That was the contrast we needed."

Lulu hired prominent Chinese actor Shuzhen Zhao to play Nai Nai, the other lead role in the film, which shot in Changchun and New York City. Lulu's great aunt played herself alongside the professional actors and in doing so gave the other actors a window into the family's experiences. Although the real Nai Nai knew her granddaughter was filming a story "about the family," she didn't know it was about her cancer diagnosis. The entire cast was part of the now six-year-old lie.

Released in summer 2019, *The Farewell* begins with Billi talking on the phone with her grandmother in China. Despite the twelve-hour time difference, this is a regular practice of these two family members who have remained close through 25 years of separation. After learning of Nai Nai's bleak diagnosis, Billi's uncle arranges a hasty wedding reception for his son and the son's Japanese fiancée, but Billi's parents don't want her to come because they believe she is "too emotional." Ever loyal to Nai Nai, Billi scrapes together the money for her own ticket and shows up in Changchun a day after her parents. The film portrays the conflict among family members—much of it in English so the elders can't understand it—as to whether to tell Nai Nai and if it's even possible to keep the news a secret.

Viewers come to understand the conflict between the collectivism ingrained in Chinese culture—a collectivism that preceded the Communist revolution by centuries if not millennia—and the American individualism that Billi and, to a great extent, her parents have embraced. When Nai Nai cannot stop coughing and briefly ends up in the hospital, Billi's father tells the family that it would be "illegal" for doctors in the United States to conceal her diagnosis from her. But Billi's uncle explains to her that the family has a "duty to carry the emotional burden" for Nai Nai by not telling her and letting her live her final days in peace.

The Teen Comedies of Amy Heckerling

Comedy has long reflected the values and experiences of people in specific times and places. Few directors have captured the lives of Gen X teenagers—those born between 1965 and 1979—better than Amy Heckerling in her comedies *Fast Times at Ridgemont High* and *Clueless*.

Heckerling, who was born in 1954 as part of the baby boomer generation, debuted with *Fast Times*, the story of a group of slacker teens in a California high school. Based on a series of articles in *Rolling Stone* by journalist Cameron Crowe, the film launched the careers of actors such as Jennifer Jason Leigh, Sean Penn, and Forest Whitaker. A critical and box-office hit, it spawned a TV series that Amy also directed.

After *Fast Times*, Amy directed several comedies about 1980s family life, including *National Lampoon's European Vacation* and *Look Who's Talking*, but she returned to the world of teenagers with the 1995 film *Clueless*. Also set in a California high school, *Clueless* stars Alicia Silverstone as the wealthy, appearance-obsessed daughter of a single father whose college-aged stepbrother shames her for her shallow materialism. She reacts by attempting "good deeds," most notably a makeover of an unpopular classmate that leads to many awkward situations.

Heckerling became disillusioned with the film industry and made few films after *Clueless*, but her pioneering teen comedies have continued to inspire young women seeking to tell the stories of their generation.

Most critics praised *The Farewell*, which took in $23 million with a production budget of $3 million. *Indiewire* reviewer Eric Kohn called it "the most exciting hit movie of the summer" and praised Lulu's decision not to include a white character to appeal to mainstream audiences. Justin Chang of the *Los Angeles Times* lauded Awkwafina and other performances and wrote, "Sidestepping the temptations of broad farce or melodrama, Wang stakes out a zone of low-key observational realism, dispensing her sympathies and teasing out emotional subtleties with a graceful, assured hand."

Awkwafina received a 2020 Golden Globe for Best Actress in a Musical or Comedy, becoming the first Asian American woman to win this award, which is given by film and TV critics. *The Farewell* received a Golden Globe nomination for Best Foreign Language Film, but despite the fact that it was a US production, it was ineligible for Best Motion Picture honors because a majority of the dialogue was not in English. These rules for the Golden Globes have come under criticism for failing to acknowledge that the immigrant experience in the United States is a multilingual one.

The Golden Globes and *Minari*

One year after *The Farewell* was nominated for a Golden Globe in the Best Foreign Language Film category, the same controversial rule afflicted *Minari*, director Lee Isaac Chung's semiautobiographical story of a Korean immigrant family trying to establish a vegetable farm in 1980s Arkansas. With more than 50 percent of the dialogue in Korean, *Minari* was disqualified for Best Motion Picture in the drama category. *Minari* was also filmed entirely in the US, making it an even stronger case for the Best Motion Picture nomination than *The Farewell* and raising questions about anti-Asian bias. In fact, two earlier films with most of their dialogue not in English—Quentin Tarantino's *Inglorious Basterds* and Alejandro González Iñárritu's *Babel*—received nominations for Best Motion Picture. *Minari* ended up winning the Golden Globe for Best Foreign Language Film in 2021.

At the time of the Golden Globes, Lulu faced a controversy of her own. The film had just opened in China with the title *Don't Tell Her*. As Lulu told *Slate*,

> [Nai Nai's] friend saw a review of it and was so proud of her, one of her longest friends, and sent it to her. . . . And so she said to little Nai Nai, her sister, who plays herself in the movie, she said, "I just thought that you were really daft, because you went and shot a movie, you went to the premiere in New York, and you come back and you can't tell me anything about it. You can't tell me what it's about. You can't tell me the title. But look, it says in the newspaper it's called *Don't Tell Her*, and that's why you didn't tell me, because I am the 'her' of the 'don't tell her.'"

In the end, Nai Nai learned of her illness through a movie seen by millions all over the world. Did the desire for

American-style success ultimately win out over the desire to "bring joy" through "the lie," as Lulu had told *Rolling Stone* a year earlier? After all, the great-aunt who orchestrated the lie was the same one who played herself in the film, knowing that if it ever opened in China, the secret would likely be revealed.

Life between two worlds, two cultures, is never simple. In making *The Farewell*, Lulu said, "I got to share the American part of my life with my family in China and the Chinese part of my life with my colleagues." The consequences of this cultural exchange, the unexpected ways it changed everyone involved, will perhaps become the subject of one of Lulu's future films.

The Making of *Nian*

Lulu has continued to explore Chinese traditions. In January 2021 she released the short film *Nian*, to coincide with the Lunar New Year. Apple funded the film to demonstrate the capabilities of the iPhone, and Lulu took on the challenge of directing a film shot entirely on this device while separated from her actors and crew in China due to COVID-19 restrictions. Available for free on YouTube, *Nian* is the story of a girl who discovers that the monsters of folktales are real but also benign if treated with kindness. The film was created to inspire budding filmmakers of all ages, especially young people who already use their smartphones to make videos on TikTok and other plaforms.

Greta Gerwig:
Forging Her Path Despite Rejection

For college-bound high school seniors, April 1 is a day of both excitement and trepidation. Past generations waited by the mailbox for envelopes: thick for acceptances, thin for rejections. Today college applicants log on to the admission website and receive the decision: ACCEPT, REJECT, WAITLIST.

Greta Gerwig's 2017 directorial debut, *Lady Bird*, for which she also wrote the screenplay, captures that day and that bittersweet year. Christine McPherson is a rule-breaking senior at a Catholic girls' high school in Sacramento, California, who insists that everyone call her Lady Bird because she hates her given name. She doesn't have the grades or the test scores to get into the elite East Coast universities she dreams of attending. Her mother wants her to attend a local college, maybe the University of California, Davis, if Lady Bird can even get in there. Her father has lost his job, and although her mother works double shifts as a nurse, they don't have the money to pay the tuition for an out-of-state or private university. Lady Bird challenges anyone in authority and is strong willed and defiant to the point of recklessness—for instance, she leaps out of the car during an argument while her mother is driving and breaks her arm. But her parents don't want her to leave home. Besides missing her, they fear she will fail if she tries to go too far.

Greta knows what it is like to go too far and fail. And she knows how to get back up and try again. Her big moment of disappointment occurred in 2006 when, as a senior at Barnard College, she applied to three prestigious master of fine arts programs in playwriting—Yale, Juilliard, and NYU—and was rejected by every one of them. Ten years later, she defended her application to Catie Lazarus on her podcast *Employee of the Month*:

> I recently went back and read the play that I had submitted, and I thought I was going to have that thing where you look back at something you wrote and you think, "Oh this was terrible. I understand." And I still thought it was pretty good. . . . It was a play about Kant and Newton as 13-year-old boys trying to date girls and debating the nature of space, and it's really funny. I don't know, I think they made a mistake.

It didn't matter whether those MFA programs had made a mistake, however. Greta was still graduating from college with her dreams of becoming a playwright crushed and no idea what she would do next. That feeling of reaching for a seemingly unattainable goal, at a time of transition from the familiar to the unknown, informs *Lady Bird*.

Greta denies that *Lady Bird* is autobiographical, though it contains many elements drawn from her own life. Greta was born on August 4, 1983, in Sacramento and, like her protagonist, graduated from a Catholic girls' high school in 2002. Her mother, Christine, worked as a nurse. Unlike Lady Bird, Greta was an excellent student, has had a close relationship with her mother as well as her father (a loan officer for a credit union), and rarely got into trouble. In a 2017 interview with critic Dana Han-Klein, Greta said, "I was more of a . . . people pleaser and a rule follower. And I think that perhaps in a way writing *Lady Bird* was sort of an unconscious unearthing of impulses I didn't know I had."

Greta began acting professionally for the first time in her senior year at Barnard. Her boyfriend at the time played one of the main characters in Joe Swanberg's low-budget film *LOL*, released in 2006, and Greta played his girlfriend. Rather than return to Sacramento or choose another industry after failing to get into graduate school, Greta remained in New York and over the next 10 years acted in films directed by Jay and Mark Duplass, Noah Baumbach, Rebecca Miller, and Pablo Larraín, among others. In addition to films, Greta acted in TV series and stage plays and did voiceovers for animation.

Through Joe Swanberg, Greta began writing for film, learning on the job rather than in school. She and Joe cowrote two films in the mumblecore genre, *Hannah Takes the Stairs*, released in 2007, and the 2008 film *Nights and Weekends*, which she also codirected with Joe.

Mumblecore

The name of this independent film genre evokes poor sound quality and hard-to-hear dialogue. Some of these aspects are true. Mumblecore films, which emerged in the mid-2000s, have small budgets, nonprofessional actors, and more dialogue than plot or action. In many instances, the actors improvise the dialogue, working from notes rather than a script. The principal characters in this genre are young people living in the city, working at first jobs, outgrowing high school and college friendships, and falling in and out of love. For a generation of teenagers who watched 1990s reality TV shows like MTV's *The Real World*, mumblecore became a way of portraying their lives in early adulthood.

Soon afterward, Greta crossed paths with writer-director Noah Baumbach, who at that time was best known for his critically acclaimed 2005 film *The Squid and the Whale*, based on his parents' divorce in Brooklyn in the 1980s and its impact on him and his brother. Greta starred in Noah's 2010 film *Greenberg*, which he wrote with his then wife, the actor Jennifer Jason Leigh. The film flopped, and Noah and Jennifer's five-year marriage ended the same year.

In 2011 Noah and Greta embarked on a collaboration that was both professional and personal. The two moved in together, and they wrote the script for *Frances Ha*. The 2012 mumblecore-inspired film, directed by Noah, established Greta as both an actor and a writer to watch.

In *Frances Ha*, Greta plays 27-year-old Frances Halliday, who wants to dance professionally, but she's clumsy, immature, and unwilling to consider another career (or any other means of supporting herself) when she is let go from the dance apprenticeship program. Her friend from college, Sophie, has moved on with her life, with a good job in publishing and a fiancé. When Sophie moves from Brooklyn to Manhattan, Frances cannot afford the apartment they've shared for years. She drifts between friends' apartments while she figures out how to reconcile her lofty dreams with her modest abilities and forge a life that makes her happy.

Although Greta is credited as the second author of the screenplay after Noah, the low-budget, black-and-white film draws deeply on her experience of rejection from graduate school and living a precarious existence far from home and family. At one point in the story, Frances visits her parents in

Sacramento—the parents in the movie played by Greta's own mother and father. Greta's performance as Frances received almost universal praise. Sarah Mink, of the feminist website Bitch Media, called *Frances Ha* "a rare and wonderful film that gives thanks for friends and revels in life's low times."

Greta first became interested in women directors when she saw Claire Denis's *Beau Travail* at Barnard. When Greta starred in the 2015 film *Maggie's Plan*, written and directed by Rebecca Miller, she realized she could direct a film herself. She had been working on the screenplay for *Lady Bird* for more than a year already, and with Rebecca's encouragement and advice, Greta set about looking for funding for the film with herself as director.

Claire Denis, Pioneer Woman Director

Born in Paris in 1946, Claire Denis emerged as a major director with her 1988 film *Chocolat*, the story of a French family living in Cameroon during the colonial era. The daughter of a civil servant, she grew up in various countries of West Africa and saw the costs of colonialism for the people of those countries and the French who ruled over them. Set among French Foreign Legion soldiers in Djibouti and released in 1999, *Beau Travail* merges Herman Melville's classic novella *Billy Budd* with Claire's perspective on French colonial rule. In recent years her work has expanded into the genres of thriller and horror.

She has served as a mentor to other women directors in France, sometimes acting in their films.

As she approached financiers for what would be her directorial debut, Greta once again had to confront rejection. It was no secret in the film industry that women have a much harder time raising money than their male counterparts. On a Times Talks panel with lead actor Saoirse Ronan and moderated by Frank Bruni, Greta said she heard a lot of "It's not for us right now" and added with a grimace, "'right now' being 'ever.'" Most of the potential investors were men, and she found that men were more receptive to her "if [they] were raised with sisters or if they had daughters." Her efforts yielded "nothing, then a lot at once," and production began.

These investors were richly rewarded with a film that not only made money but also achieved one of the all-time highest ratings on the movie review aggregator Rotten Tomatoes. *Lady Bird* was nominated for five Academy Awards, and Greta was the first woman to receive an Academy Award nomination for Best Director in her solo debut film. *Lady Bird* won a Golden Globe for Best Motion Picture in the musical or comedy category, and Saoirse won the Golden Globe for Best Actress.

Greta gives credit to more experienced women directors for her early acclaim. When she acted for the French director Mia Hansen-Løve on the 2014 film *Eden*, Greta learned to ignore critics who attributed her success to her romantic or family connections. Like Greta, Mia had started out acting for a famous filmmaker, Olivier Assayas, and had become his partner. Greta remembers a pivotal story from Mia:

> [Mia] said that the other young male writers . . . treated her dismissively because they thought of her as Olivier's girlfriend, who got there because she was his girlfriend, and how they changed when she had her first movie at Cannes, when she was in her 20s. All of a sudden they looked at her like they'd never seen her before. I hung onto that story. All those little pieces I put in my pocket. I think I needed these little signs.

Greta's Mentors: Mia Hansen-Løve, Rebecca Miller, and Sofia Coppola

When critics credited Greta's partner, Noah Baumbach, for writing *Frances Ha*, minimizing her contributions, she found herself in the company of other women filmmakers who have faced similar challenges because of their family ties. These women inspired and mentored Greta as she moved from acting to screenwriting to directing films. French-born Mia Hansen-Løve came into her own with *Father of My Children*, the Jury Special Prize winner at the 2009 Cannes Film Festival. She was only 28 years old at the time. Since then, she has directed five films that have garnered international acclaim, with one more in the works.

Rebecca Miller is the daughter of the acclaimed American playwright and essayist Arthur Miller and the wife of the knighted English actor Daniel Day-Lewis. Born in 1962, she studied art and filmmaking but began her professional career in the late 1980s as an actor for stage, film, and television. She released her first film, *Angela*, in 1995. She directed five more feature films afterward, including the 2015 romantic comedy *Maggie's Plan*. In it, Greta plays a single woman who wants to have a child and has arranged to be artificial inseminated via a guy friend—named Guy—but then meets John, an author struggling with a novel and a bad marriage. Rebecca's mentorship played a critical role in Greta becoming a director and later directing a film adaptation of a work of literature, as Rebecca did in *Maggie's Plan* and much of her other work. In addition to acting and directing, Rebecca is an author of award-winning books. She has directed adaptations of her essay collection *Personal Velocity* and her novel *The Private Lives of Pippa Lee* for film.

While Greta has not yet worked directly with Sofia Coppola, she talks about meeting Sofia at festivals and sharing experiences of being a woman in the film industry. Born in 1971, Sofia is the daughter of one of the most important American film directors, Francis Ford Coppola, who is most famous for *The Godfather* trilogy. While he opened doors for Sofia to act in her childhood and financed her projects, this also led to charges of nepotism. Despite the tendency of critics to dismiss her work, Sofia has established herself as a major writer and director in her own right with her films *The Virgin Suicides* (1999), *Lost in Translation* (2003), *Marie Antoinette* (2006), *The Beguiled* (2017), and more. With *Lost in Translation*, she became the third woman ever to receive an Academy Award nomination for Best Director, and she ended up with the Oscar for Best Original Screenplay.

When Greta worked on *Lady Bird*, she wore shoes that writer-directors Rebecca Miller and Miranda July had given her as a symbol of their support. She, in turn, has expressed her desire to mentor younger woman filmmakers, including Saoirse, who also starred in Greta's adaptation of *Little Women*. In the Times Talks panel, Greta spoke of "too many" talented women seeking to direct films. But "too many" didn't mean too much competition over opportunities but rather too many women for a male-dominated industry to ignore. In other words, each talented woman director creates opportunities for others.

This idea of talented women lifting up each other informed Greta's vision for her adaptation of Louisa May Alcott's 19th-century classic, *Little Women*, released in 2019. Greta gave *Little Women* more feminist overtones than previous adaptations, focusing not only on Jo's ambition but also on her efforts to make her sisters' dreams come true. She helps her sisters—and they help her—even though they also fight and do terrible things to each other.

Like *Lady Bird*, *Little Women* received critical praise. It was nominated for six Academy Awards, including Best Picture and Best Adapted Screenplay. It was a surprise moneymaker as well; with a production budget of $40 million, the film grossed almost $200 million worldwide and netted $56 million in profits.

Greta emerged as a director during the era of #MeToo. Though the Me Too movement originated from Tarana Burke in 2006, the hashtag rose to prominence in 2017 with revelations of producer Harvey Weinstein's decades-long abuse of women. Along with mentoring the young women she works with, Greta has sought to create a safe environment for them. Above all, she wants young women to seek opportunities themselves and not wait for men to open the door for them. Key to that is mentorship by women who have already attained success and the confidence that comes with it.

Most great movies begin with great writing. *Frances Ha*, *Lady Bird*, and *Little Women* are examples. None of these films were expected to find large audiences or earn a lot of money. But when they opened, strong reviews and word of mouth led to growing audiences in the following weeks.

Despite every MFA playwriting program rejecting her, Greta received an Academy Award nomination for Best Original Screenplay for *Lady Bird* and a Best Adapted Screenplay nomination for *Little Women*. Even though she did not win either prize, being nominated means her writing was in the top five of all screenplays that year. It's only a matter of time before this talented writer and director takes home the golden statue.

Issa Rae: From Awkward Black Girl to Hollywood Mogul

Black and awkward? These two adjectives would become the catalyst for Issa Rae's illustrious career in the entertainment industry. Born Jo-Issa Rae Diop in Los Angeles, California, on January 12, 1985, she is the third of five children. Issa's family somewhat mirrored the Cosbys, her dad a doctor and her mom an educator. In 1988 her parents decided to move from the Golden State to her father's birthplace, Dakar, Senegal. For about two and half years, her dad attempted to establish a hospital in his hometown but was unsuccessful in the venture.

Once they realized that the hospital wasn't going to happen, the family moved back to the United States to Potomac, Maryland, where they stayed until the end of Issa's fifth-grade year. For those few years in Potomac, she had a group of diverse friends and wasn't considered an outsider. "Growing up as a young black girl in Potomac, Maryland, was easy. I had a Rainbow Coalition of friends of all ethnicities, and we would carelessly skip around our elementary school like the powerless version of Captain Planet's Planeteers." Besides, not knowing how to dance like some Black girls wasn't a factor during that time. "I never really had to put much thought into my race and neither did anybody else. I knew I was black. I knew there was a history that accompanied my skin color and my parents taught me to be proud of it."

However, things changed when her dad was offered an opportunity to set up a new pediatric practice back in Los Angles. Initially she was excited about the move back to her birthplace, but moving before the start of middle school can be a life-altering experience. Depending on the person, grades six through eight can be the catalyst of self-discovery and self-worth. "I remember being excited about the house we were going to buy in California because it was significantly bigger, and I felt like we were going to have a bigger life," Issa said in an interview with the *Washington Post*.

Issa was an incredibly gifted student. Her mother being an educator probably helped, and Issa's stellar grades afforded her the chance to attend the prestigious Stanford University. But after the move to L.A., her success in the classroom no longer extended to her social life. She quickly learned that things that were celebrated in Maryland were questioned by her young Californian peers. Suddenly the way she talked and dressed and even her sense of her humor were deemed not Black enough for her new friends. "Who I was was not acceptable to black L.A. youth: the way I spoke and my sense of humor," Issa said. "Everybody else had relaxers and pressed hair. I wore my hair in an Afro puff. Nappy. The way I dressed. It was all about name brands at the time in L.A. I had no idea. All those things, I failed miserably at."

Those same sentiments stayed with her at her private high school, where she would try to prove her Blackness to her white classmates. She recalled in a personal essay for *HuffPost* a time in the eighth grade when she and another classmate began to argue about the dopeness of Sean Combs, who at the time was known as Puff Daddy. Naturally, the classmate, who was a white boy, disagreed with her assertions and countered back with a rap artist that Issa was unfamiliar with. Determined to stake her claim on the hill that Puff Daddy was in fact an amazing rapper at the time, Issa quickly found herself in a losing battle against him. Her Blackness had been reduced to her rap knowledge—or lack thereof—and she had been one-upped by someone who didn't even share the same skin color or ethnic background.

As she got older and began to take an interest and pride in her heritage as a Black woman, she "realized there was more to being black than a knowledge of rap music, and that I didn't have to live up to this pop cultural archetype." Issa said, "I began to take pride in the fact that I wasn't a stereotype and that I didn't have to be."

Issa grew up in a renaissance of Black-focused media, which gave her a safe space to enjoy Black culture. During the 90s there was an explosion of shows that highlighted Black people in a positive light and offered the representation still begging to be seen in mainstream media today. For instance, *A Different World* showed life at a historically Black college through the lens of its dynamic characters and gave a sense of pride in education. "*A Different World* made me want to go to college, talk about smart-black-people stuff, and find my own Dwayne Wayne." This was a time when a person of color could relate to the images being shown, aspire to become more, and be entertained. Because of media like *A Different World*, Issa found herself able to learn and relate more to Black culture. So when her classmates teased her about having nappy hair and talking white, Issa found "a sort of solace in knowing that Freddie from *A Different World* and Sinclair from *Living Single* were napped out, too. I could be worse things."

Around the same time that Issa and her family had moved back to Los Angeles, her love for writing kicked in. As she shares in her bestselling book, *The Misadventures of Awkward Black Girl*, "I was in the hub of film and television and felt a need to take advantage of this, as quickly as possible"—so much so that she wrote her first spec script when the new Cosby show aired, when she was only 11 years old. She showed the script to her grandmother, who encouraged her to send it into CBS, the network that was carrying the show. Her script centered around a family grappling with the fact that their daughter had gotten a tongue piercing. Apparently, a young Issa thought that was a pretty controversial thing for a teen to do at that time. Without a second thought, she sent off the script and didn't worry about if the network would love it or not. Spoiler alert: it didn't, but it was kind with its rejection. Not deterred by the denial, she continued to write more scripts and send them out to various networks.

By the time she reached high school, Issa had also fallen in love with acting and participated in the theater program at her high school. Because the school was predominately Black and Latino, it offered her the opportunity to be fully immersed in Black culture. Issa credits her drama teacher for inspiring her and exposing her to various plays written by people of color. "Every year for four years I was introduced to new diverse works, all while working with a multicultural cast. I only wish Hollywood could take a lesson from Compton." Then she saw *Love & Basketball*, directed and written by Gina Prince-Bythewood—an African American woman! Seeing the movie and learning about Gina helped spark a newfound love for film and writing for movies.

However, by the time she had reached Stanford, she had started to lose her excitement for theater. She quickly learned that she didn't fit in with Stanford's theater department. At the time, all the plays were written by white people, and the leads cast were white as well. But before her faith completely dissipated, a classmate named Debi created a hip-hopera and made Issa one of the leads. Energized by her role in the play, she decided to take her talents backstage. Issa tried her hand at directing a stage version of Spike Lee's *School Daze*. "Looking back, I had no idea what I was doing, but directing and producing gave me a sense of control that I didn't have as an actress." These experiences allowed her to realize that, one way or another, "Stanford gave me the opportunity to put my own spin on theater, and to learn by doing."

While she loved directing and producing plays—which were a hit with the other students at Stanford—she needed to finish her last two quarters to earn her degree on time. She took a couple of courses at her local community college to finish her degree in African American studies. To help her cope with the stress of completing her college career, she created her first web series called *Dorm Diaries*, highlighting her experience as a Black student at Stanford. It was during her time there that she learned that Black people are not monolithic but very diverse, which was refreshing for her to witness.

Despite the success of *Dorm Diaries*, she was still frustrated with the lack of positive images of Black people and people of color in mainstream media. All the shows and movies from the '90s that highlighted Black folks in such a positive light had been slowly replaced with reality television shows that seemed to show Black people, and Black women especially, in the worst light. "How hard is it to portray a three-dimensional woman of color on television or in film? I'm surrounded by them. They're my friends. I talk to them to every day," she wrote in her book. She wondered if Hollywood regarded Black women as a joke, not worthy of the same depth as other ethnic groups.

After graduating from Stanford, she took an internship in New York with a theater company. While on Facebook one day, "it came to me I was awkward and black. I thought the combination was funny. . . . I wrote it as my Facebook status: I'm awkward and black." One her friends commented on the status, "Awkward and black are the two worst things a person could be." Issa knew that in order to combat her growing pessimistic attitude regarding Hollywood, she would need to do something. Enter the YouTube revolution and the birth of her next web series, aptly titled *Awkward Black Girl—ABG* for short.

Issa was onto something with *ABG*, and she was creating a character not normally seen on television: Black and awkward. If the character did exist—Steve Urkel, anyone?—they were always the sidekick that was the butt of all jokes, never the lead. YouTube allowed her the opportunity to showcase her new idea in exactly the way that she wanted to. As she shared in her book, if *ABG* had become a cable network show, "I would have been indefinitely discouraged by the network executive who suggested that actor / video girl / Lil Wayne's baby's mother, Lauren London, would be a great fit for the title character of a cable version of *Awkward Black Girl*." She took it a step further, writing,

> If it weren't for social media, I don't know that black women would even be a fully formed blip on the radar. If it weren't for internet forums and fan pages, communities of dark women wouldn't be empowered by their natural hair in a media society that tells them their hair should be straightened and their skin should be lighter.

In 2011 *ABG* launched on YouTube and eventually became a viral sensation. The show portrays its main character, J, played by Issa herself, in awkward situations created by her coworkers and love interests. It was her goal to have a show that was the Black version of *30 Rock*, *Seinfeld*, and *Friends*. She noted how shows like *Girls*, *New Girl*, and *2 Broke Girls* all had something in common: "The universal gender classification, "girl," is white. . . . That is the norm and that is what is acceptable. Anything else is niche." Each episode of *ABG* was about 15 minutes long, much to the disappointment of its fans. However, that didn't stop people from waiting patiently—or impatiently—for the next episode to be released on YouTube. The web series soon caught the eye of television networks, and talks began about bringing her vision from the internet to television screens.

But in true Hollywood fashion, most of the networks wanted to change her vision of the show. As she recalled in an interview with *New York Times Magazine*, "A phone conversation with a network executive who wanted to make it into a pan-racial franchise operation, starting with 'Awkward Indian Boy.'" But she didn't fault the networks for trying to rework the show into something that felt more palatable for its audience. After being in the entertainment industry for a while, she started to understand that marginalizing media is not always blatant racism like she once believed. "It's more complicated than that. . . . We're simply not on their radar. As long as the people who are in charge aren't us, things will never change."

She almost caught a huge break when Shonda Rhimes and her team received a pitch from Issa called "I Hate L.A. Dudes." Shonda loved the pitch so much that she and one of her show runners, Betsy Beers, was able to sell it ABC. Everything was going well until communication started to break down between the parties. Issa had trouble getting her script ready in time for the upcoming winter pilot season and ended up falling short of the network's expectations. "I compromised my vision, and it didn't end up the show that I wanted," she said in her interview with *New York Times Magazine*. "It wasn't funny anymore."

But before she could lick her wounds, the network executives from HBO came calling, looking to work with her on a different project. In 2013 she pitched to them a concept called "Insecure." Intrigued by the premise of the show, HBO worked with her for over a year before the network finally accepted a script from her. Prior to its acceptance, each of the scripts she had written at that time kept getting shot down by the network. She couldn't help but feel as if maybe this wasn't what she was supposed to be doing. Even with her mentor, Larry Wilmore, she still couldn't seem to meet the expectations of the network. Things really seemed bleak when she got a call from HBO letting her know that the last script wasn't it either and that her mentor was being reassigned. "I remember being on the set of a pilot we were filming and getting the call that HBO was not feeling the latest draft and I was losing Larry. I was like, 'This isn't going to happen for me, and I just did all of this for nothing.'"

At first Issa was a bit disappointed to not have the comfort of her mentor beside her anymore, but it turned out his leaving was a blessing in disguise. His departure helped her to shift her focus from what she thought the show was about—an office-place comedy—to what she really wanted it to be about—a young Black millennial woman navigating life. With Larry gone and another conversation with HBO regarding the new direction of the show, a spark within was ignited. "It was just like, 'I'm going to put everything that I'm going through out on the table in this pilot. If they say no, at least I tried, and f— it.'"

The pilot episode of *Insecure* aired on HBO in October 2016 to a warm reception from fans and critics. The show centered on a African American woman in her late 20s, navigating her relationships, friendships, and career, all while representing and showcasing Issa Rae's hometown of L.A. Issa plays the main character, Issa Dee, who is loosely based on her real life.

Ten years later Issa has made an impressive name for herself within Hollywood. Her breakout show on HBO, *Insecure*, earned a whopping eight Emmy nominations in 2020. She also received an eight-figure, five-year deal with WarnerMedia, which offers the network an exclusive look at her new projects. Issa's dedication to creating media that normalizes Black life should be celebrated, and her efforts are something we can enjoy for years to come. Issa Rae is the quintessential Black nerd.

Nia DaCosta: Age Ain't Nothing but a Number

Candyman. Candyman. Candyman. Candyman. Candy—

In 1992 one of the most iconic and horrifying films was released in movie theaters across the United States. *Candyman* centers around a Black man who was murdered for having a forbidden interracial love affair and now exists as a supernatural entity who kills anyone who says his name five times in the mirror. The year it was released, Nia DaCosta was only two years old and didn't yet have filmmaking and storytelling on her little toddler mind.

In 27 years, she would be tapped to direct the remake of *Candyman* underneath Jordan Peele's production company, Monkeypaw Productions. Before Nia arrived at this pivotal moment in her life, her love for film directing was heavily influenced by Martin Scorsese, a highly regarded and seasoned film director, and she attended the renowned New York University's Tisch School of the Arts, just like her hero. While attending NYU, she discovered that she also enjoyed writing and telling stories in her own way, as much as she did directing movies.

After she left New York, she travelled to London to obtain her master of fine arts from the Royal Central School of Speech and Drama in London, England. While pursuing her degree, she found herself immersed in the culture of theater, which is much bigger in that part of the world than in the US. By the time she came back to the United States, Nia was ready to get to work.

With a script developed while working as a television production assistant after graduate school, Nia was one out of twelve submissions to be chosen to participate in the Sundance Institute Directors and Screenwriters Labs program. This enabled her to film her first project, *Little Woods*, which takes place in rural North Dakota and stars Tessa Thompson and Lily James. The movie highlighted the inequality and disparate class treatment of the health care system. She shared in an interview with the *Wall Street Journal*, "I'm definitely interested in class and how it represents itself in our culture, and how, depending on where you live, your life can be very different," she said. "With *Little Woods*, it was interesting to realize that [even though] I grew up with not a lot of money in New York City—my situation was different to a woman growing up with not a lot of money in a rural part of America because of the access to services."

It's not surprising that when she was asked to direct the remake of *Candyman* she would want to root it in modern issues. She pointed out in the same interview with the *Wall Street Journal*,

> As a Black woman growing up, you slowly but surely learn you're Black . . . and the earliest instance of what that meant for me was when Amadou Diallo was shot at 41 times by the NYPD in 1999, and none of the officers were convicted. Every time another Black person is killed by the police, I remember Amadou Diallo, and this movie connects to that: I can't stop thinking about how, in the first film, Candyman was an artist, killed by a white mob, *before* he was a murderous ghost with a hook. I wanted to explore and expand on that mythology— [while] still being thrilling and scary and fun and all the things horror needs to be.

But more than anything, Nia aims to show Black people in more diverse roles. As she told *Variety*, "The lack of imagination for people of color in such an imaginative world is disappointing." She continued, "We can imagine dragons and zombies and all this amazing stuff, and people of color just don't exist, or even women being not a princess in the genre."

Despite *Candyman* being delayed till August 27, 2021, Nia received an offer in 2020 to direct a movie even bigger than *Candyman*. The behemoth known as the Marvel Cinematic Universe came to her about directing the next installment of the Captain Marvel series, putting her on the same level as other women directors like Gina Prince-Bythewood, Chloé Zhao, and Ava DuVernay. It is safe to assume that she will have a lot of flexibility—and money—to make sure the new Captain Marvel movie, *The Marvels*, lives up to all the glorious hype that comes with making a Marvel movie.

Acknowledgments

Lyn

Living in New York City has made it possible for me to see all kinds of independent and international films. While the COVID-19 pandemic shut down theaters for more than a year, many venues pivoted to online showings and Zoom panels that brought filmmakers from around the world into everyone's living room. And when the theaters and festivals resumed, we saw what outstanding work had been done despite the obstacles. I would especially like to thank the Film Forum, IFC, the Metrograph, the New York Film Festival, and the Polish Cultural Institute for their programming and special events that I was able to attend online and in person.

My late husband, Richard Lachmann, accompanied me to many of these films, and we discussed the work of the various filmmakers included in this volume. I am sorry he won't see the finished book, but it bears his input and his wisdom.

I thank my awesome agent, Jacqui Lipton, for thinking of me for this project (maybe because I wanted to talk about movies with her all the time) and for bringing it to Chicago Review Press. Thank you to Kara Rota and her team—copyeditor and project editor Frances Giguette and cover and interior artist Sadie Teper—who have created this inspiring series and made our work shine. We couldn't have done it without the filmmakers themselves—the pioneers and the ones who carried the work forward and created opportunities unimaginable a century ago.

Finally, I would like to thank my coauthor, Tanisia "Tee" Moore, for being a fun and thoughtful collaborator from beginning to end. I have learned so much from working with you, Tee, and am so proud of what we created together.

Tee

As always, I want to thank God for blessing me with such an incredible gift. It is my prayer that I use it in the way You intended, bringing You glory and honor.

To my parents and siblings, thank you for all your support and encouragement over the years.

To my husband and kiddos, I know the road hasn't always been easy, but thanks for hanging in there with me. Love y'all.

To my best writing friends/family—Ebony, Winsome, Kenneth, Allen, Antwan, and Tonya (Da' Crew)—a gal could ask for, love y'all. To my wonderful critique partners, who acted as a sounding board and kept me sane in this process— Tanisha, Monica, and James—thanks for letting me in the circle. I appreciate y'all so much. And to my ladies who just get me—Jas, Janelle, Stacey, Ashley, Maisha, and Shana—love y'all, and thank you so much for being on this journey with me.

To my amazing and outstanding agent and friend, Jemiscoe, you really are a gem. I appreciate you for taking an interest not only in my work but also in me. I'm honored to be a Hologram.

To my coauthor, Lyn, thank you for being patient, kind, and uplifting throughout this process. You're such an inspiration, and I'm happy to have done this project with you.

To my editor, Kara, and the team at Chicago Review Press, I appreciate this opportunity to be a part of this dynamic series.

To the women in this book, thank you for showing up with your talent and sharing your gift with the world. You reminded me that I'm necessary in this space.

Lastly, to _____ (put your name here), thank you so much for all your support, encouragement, and love! You have made this journey so much better.

Xoxo,

Tee

Selected Filmography

Jane Campion

The Power of the Dog (feature film, 2021)
Top of the Lake (TV series, 2013-2017)
The Piano (feature film, 1993)
An Angel at My Table (feature film, 1990)
Sweetie (feature film, 1989)

Agnieszka Holland

Mr. Jones (feature film, 2019)
Spoor (feature film, 2017)
Burning Bush (TV miniseries, 2013)
Treme (TV series, five episodes, 2010-2013)
In Darkness (feature film, 2011)
The Secret Garden (feature film, 1993)
Europa Europa (feature film, 1990)

Kathryn Bigelow

Detroit (feature film, 2017)
Zero Dark Thirty (feature film, 2012)
The Hurt Locker (feature film, 2008)
K-19: The Widowmaker (feature film, 2002)
Point Break (feature film, 1991)

Ava DuVernay

When They See Us (TV miniseries, 2019)
A Wrinkle in Time (feature film, 2018)
13th (documentary feature, 2016)
Queen Sugar (TV series, two episodes, 2016)
Selma (feature film, 2014)

Regina King

One Night in Miami (feature film, 2020)
Insecure (TV series, one episode, 2018)
This Is Us (TV series, one episode, 2017)
Being Mary Jane (TV series, six episodes, 2015)
Southland (TV series, one episode, 2013)

Shonda Rhimes

Scandal (TV series, creator and showrunner, 2012–2018)

Grey's Anatomy (TV series, creator, 2005–present; showrunner, 2005–2017)

The Princess Diaries 2: Royal Engagement (feature film, screenplay, 2004)

Introducing Dorothy Dandridge (TV movie, 1999)

Gina Prince-Bythewood

The Old Guard (feature film, 2020)

Beyond the Lights (feature film, 2014)

The Secret Life of Bees (feature film, 2008)

Disappearing Acts (TV movie, 2000)

Love & Basketball (feature film, 2000)

Kimberly Peirce

Carrie (feature film, 2013)

Stop-Loss (feature film, 2008)

Boys Don't Cry (feature film, 1999)

Dee Rees

The Last Thing He Wanted (feature film, 2020)

Mudbound (feature film, 2017)

Bessie (TV movie, 2015)

Pariah (feature film, 2011)

Chloé Zhao

Eternals (feature film, 2021)
Nomadland (feature film, 2020)
The Rider (feature film, 2017)
Songs My Brother Taught Me (feature film, 2015)

Petra Costa

The Edge of Democracy (documentary feature, 2019)
Olmo and the Seagull (documentary feature, codirected with Lea Glob, 2015)
Elena (documentary feature, 2012)

Mindy Kaling

Never Have I Ever (TV series, cocreator; writer, three episodes; 2020–present)
The Mindy Project (TV series, creator; writer, 25 episodes; 2012–2017)
Mindy and Brenda (TV movie, 2006)
The Office (TV series, writer, 27 episodes, 2005–2012)

Lulu Wang

Nian (short film, 2021)

The Farewell (feature film, 2019)
Posthumous (feature film, 2014)

Greta Gerwig

Little Women (feature film, 2019)
Lady Bird (feature film, 2017)

Issa Rae

Insecure (TV series, creator; writer, nine episodes; 2016–2021)
The Misadventures of Awkward Black Girl (TV series short, creator, 2011–2013)

Notes

Introduction

"women comprised 21%":Martha M. Lauzen, "The Celluloid Ceiling: Behind-the-Scenes Employment of Women on the Top U.S. Films of 2020," Celluloid Ceiling Report, Center for the Study of Women in Television and Film, San Diego State University, 2021, https://womenintvfilm.sdsu.edu/wp-content/uploads/2021/01/2020_Celluloid_Ceiling_Report.pdf.

"a personnel database": Kate Erbland, "Ava DuVernay: True Success for Inclusive ARRAY Database Will Be When It's No Longer Needed," *Indiewire*, March 19, 2021, https://www.indiewire.com/2021/03/ava-duvernay-array-crew-database-1234624854/.

"First. Only. Different.": Shonda Rhimes, *Year of Yes: How to Dance It Out, Stand in the Sun and Be Your Own Person* (New York: Simon and Schuster, 2016), 138.

1. Jane Campion

Following the collapse: Alistair Fox, *Jane Campion: Authorship and Personal Cinema* (Bloomington: Indiana University Press, 2011).

she "just thought, in the most unconscious fashion": Katherine Dieckmann and Michael Tabb, "New Again: Jane Campion," *Interview*, May 30, 2012, first published January 1992, https://www.interviewmagazine.com/film/new-again-jane-campion.

"I always loved Emily Brontë's imagination": Kate Muir, "Jane Campion: 'Capitalism Is Such a Macho Force. I Felt Run Over,'" *Guardian*, May 20, 2018, https://www.theguardian.com/film/2018/may/20/jane-campion-unconventional-film-maker-macho-force.

Notes

She has noted that since the 1980s: Fox, *Jane Campion*.

"a spectacular feature-film debut": Vincent Canby, "Film Festival; 'Sweetie,' a Wry Comedy by New Australian Director," *New York Times*, October 6, 1989.

"I found the whole Cannes thing": Myra Forsberg, "FILM; 'Sweetie' Isn't Sugary," *New York Times*, January 14, 1990.

"strangely engrossing": Roger Ebert, "An Angel at My Table," RogerEbert.com, June 21, 1991, https://www.rogerebert.com/reviews/an-angel-at-my-table-1991.

"was this massive female filmmaker fest": Jean Bentley, "From an Oscar at 11 to 'Flack': The 25-Year Career Evolution of Anna Paquin," *Hollywood Reporter*, February 21, 2019, https://www.hollywoodreporter.com/tv/tv-news/evolution-anna-paquin-1188324/.

"as peculiar and haunting": Roger Ebert, "The Piano," RogerEbert.com, November 19, 1993, https://www.rogerebert.com/reviews/the-piano-1993.

"The film looks deceptively small": Vincent Canby, "Review/Film Festival; Forceful Lessons of Love and Cinematic Language," *New York Times*, October 16, 1993.

"I really didn't enjoy": Muir, "Jane Campion: Capitalism."

"I was going to take a break": Simon Hattenstone, "Jane Campion: 'The Clever People Used To Do Film. Now They Do TV,'" *Guardian*, July 22, 2017, https://www.theguardian.com/film/2017/jul/22/jane-campion-clever-people-film-tv-top-of-the-lake.

"I think she's fantastic": Emma Rawson, "Alice Englert Talks About Her Mum Jane Campion and Top of the Lake: China Girl," *thisNZlife* (blog), https://thisnzlife.co.nz/alice-englert-mum-jane-campion-top-lake-china-girl/.

"Cinema in Australia": Hattenstone, "Clever People Used to Do Film."

"I think power is always": Rebecca Keegan, "Jane Campion on 'The Power of the Dog's Toxic Masculinity and Why She Won't Make a Marvel Movie," *Hollywood Reporter*, September 10, 2021, https://www.hollywoodreporter.com/movies/movie-features/jane-campion-the-power-of-the-dog-interview-1235010819/.

power "comes through": Keegan, "'The Power of the Dog"s Toxic Masculinity."

2. Agnieszka Holland

"thinking about Poland": Mai Jones Jeromski, "13 Reasons Hollywood Loves Agnieszka Holland," Culture.pl, November 17, 2018, https:// culture.pl/en/article/13-reasons-hollywood-loves-agnieszka-holland.

"Certainly the mystery of my father's": Roger Cohen, "Holland Without a Country," *New York Times Magazine*, August 8, 1993, https://www .nytimes.com/1993/08/08/magazine/holland-without-a-country.html.

"a genre deeply entrenched": Jeromski, "Hollywood Loves Agnieszka Holland."

"It was eight months": Cohen, "Holland Without a Country."

"It was very costly": Larry Rohter, "To Tell a Dark Tale, Avoid Bright Stars," *New York Times*, December 2, 2011, https://www.nytimes.com /2011/12/04/movies/agnieszka-hollands-holocaust-feature-in -darkness.html.

"I found it crucial": Larry Rohter, "In the Sewers with 'In Darkness,'" *The Carpetbagger* (blog), *New York Times*, February 3, 2012, https:// carpetbagger.blogs.nytimes.com/2012/02/03/in-the-sewers-with-in -darkness/.

"a fine adaptation": Nell Minow, "The Secret Garden," Common Sense Media, last modified April 27, 2020, https://www.commonsensemedia .org/movie-reviews/the-secret-garden.

worked with the animals: Kasia Adamik, Q and A with Kasia Adamik and Agnieszka Holland on *Spoor* at 55th New York Film Festival, Alice Tully Hall, September 30, 2017.

"a deeply anti-Christian": Kate Connolly, "Agnieszka Holland: Pokot Reflects Divided Nature of Polish Society." *Guardian*, February 16, 2017, https://www.theguardian.com/film/2017/feb/16/agnieszka -holland-pokot-reflects-divided-nature-of-polish-society.

"television became much more innovative": Alastair McKay, "Drama Queen: Agnieszka Holland on the TV revolution." BBC, April 18, 2016, https:// www.bbc.co.uk/programmes/articles/4rcy2qbj5Qjdqw6hnpW8mxj /drama-queen-agnieszka-holland-on-the-tv-revolution.

3. Kathryn Bigelow

"Well, the time has come": "Kathryn Bigelow Wins Best Directing: 2010 Oscars," Oscars, YouTube video, 5:50, uploaded March 10, 2020, https://www.youtube.com/watch?v=e-DPBOTlSWk.

As she stated in a 60 Minutes: Kathryn Bigelow, "Kathryn Bigelow," interview by Leslie Stahl, CBS, YouTube video, 13:09, uploaded July 12, 2010, https://www.youtube.com/watch?v=rqY0WWV93to.

While the film fictionalized events: "K-19 Première Divides Russians," BBC News, October 7, 2002, http://news.bbc.co.uk/2/hi/entertainment /2305541.stm.

"As a member of the general public": Kathryn Bigelow and Mark Boal, "Kathryn Bigelow and Mark Boal Discuss Their Latest Film 'The Hurt Locker,'" interview by the Associated Press, AP Archive, YouTube video, 5:54, uploaded February 12, 2021, originally uploaded October 13, 2009, https://www.youtube.com/watch?v=QNNNapxY6ZY.

"I'm drawn to provocative characters": Kathryn Bigelow, "Kathryn Bigelow on The Hurt Locker," interview by Jason Solomons, The Guardian, YouTube video, 9:07, uploaded August 26, 2009, https://www.youtube .com/watch?v=TTmw_gxzWP4.

"both as antiwar and as a tribute": Bigelow, "Kathryn Bigelow," Stahl.

"If 'The Hurt Locker' is not": A. O. Scott, "Soldiers on a Live Wire Between Peril and Protocol," *New York Times*, June 25, 2009.

"Bigelow says more about the agony": Peter Bradshaw, "The Hurt Locker," *Guardian*, August 28, 2009, https://www.theguardian.com/film/2009 /aug/28/the-hurt-locker-review.

"a great film, an intelligent film": Roger Ebert, "The Most Dangerous Job in the Army," RogerEbert.com, July 8, 2009, revised July 11, 2009, https://www.rogerebert.com/reviews/the-hurt-locker-2009.

"undaunted by any potential": Bigelow and Boal, "Katherine Bigelow and Mark Boal Discuss."

"brilliantly directed . . . a cool": Manohla Dargis, "By Any Means Necessary," *New York Times*, December 17, 2012.

"sticks solemnly": Peter Bradshaw, "Zero Dark Thirty—Review," *Guardian*, January 24, 2013, https://www.theguardian.com/film/2013/jan/24 /zero-dark-thirty-review.

"Torture does not work": John McCain, "McCain Slams 'Zero Dark Thirty,'" interview by Wolf Blitzer, *The Situation Room*, CNN, YouTube video, 2:40, uploaded December 20, 2012, https://www.youtube.com/watch?v=CZZhhpG8sq4.

"To have eliminated it": Kathryn Bigelow, "Kathryn Bigelow Discusses Controversial Torture Scene in Zero Dark Thirty," interview by Peter Travers, ABC News, YouTube video, 9:08, uploaded January 11, 2013, https://www.youtube.com/watch?v=hRnFcr7JeKg.

"As a lifelong pacifist": Kathryn Bigelow, "Kathryn Bigelow Addresses 'Zero Dark Thirty' Torture Criticism," *Los Angeles Times*, January 15, 2013, https://www.latimes.com/entertainment/movies/la-xpm-2013-jan-15-la-et-mn-0116-bigelow-zero-dark-thirty-20130116-story.html.

Lead actor John Boyega: Kate Erbland, "John Boyega Defends 'Detroit' Director Kathryn Bigelow Against Backlash," *Indiewire*, August 2, 2017, https://www.indiewire.com/2017/08/john-boyega-defends-detroit-director-kathryn-bigelow-1201862561/.

Interviewed along with Kathryn: Kathryn Bigelow and Anthony Mackie, "Director Kathryn Bigelow, Actor Anthony Mackie Talk Race Relations and New Film 'Detroit,'" interview by CBS This Morning, CBS Mornings, YouTube video, 6:22, uploaded July 28, 2017, https://www.youtube.com/watch?v=16jzsiozPMk.

"I think the idea": Bigelow, "Kathryn Bigelow" Stahl.

4. Ava DuVernay

"My mom would go to work": Geoff Edgers, "The Ava Effect," *Washington Post*, Feb. 15, 2018, https://www.washingtonpost.com/news/style/wp/2018/02/15/feature/why-ava-duvernay-is-exactly-what-we-need-right-now/.

"When you walked in": Ava DuVernay, "Ava DuVernay Can't Stop, Won't Stop," interview by Geoff Edgers, *Edge of Fame* (podcast), WBUR, Feb. 14, 2018, https://www.wbur.org/geoffedgers/2018/02/15/ava-duvernay-oprah-wrinkle-in-time-metoo.

"My mother would": Edgers, "Ava Effect."

"I've watched over 200": Ava DuVernay, "Ava DuVernay Gives Career

Advice," interview by Reese Witherspoon, Reese Witherspoon x Hello Sunshine, YouTube video, 3:59, July 18, 2018, https://www.youtube.com/watch?v=ojd8hqYx7Hw.

"[Colin Tervorrow] is the whipping boy": Edgers, "Ava Effect."

"Take that desperation": DuVernay, "Ava DuVernay Can't Stop."

"Never heard of it": DuVernay, "Ava DuVernay Can't Stop."

"All of those guys": Edgers, "Ava Effect."

It should also be noted that both movies: Pamela McClintock, "A Wrinkle in Time: Why Has It Underperformed at the Box Office?," *Hollywood Reporter*, March 13, 2018, https://www.hollywoodreporter.com/movies/movie-news/a-wrinkle-time-why-it-has-underperformed-at-box-office-1094032/.

"The villain is the darkness": Melena Ryzik, "Ava DuVernay's Fiercely Feminine Vision for 'A Wrinkle in Time,'" *New York Times*, March 1, 2018, https://www.nytimes.com/2018/03/01/movies/a-wrinkle-in-time-ava-duvernay-disney.html.

"I'm conscious of the fact": Ava DuVernay, "How 'Wrinkle in Time' Director Ava DuVernay Is Breaking Down Walls in Hollywood," interview by Jeffrey Brown, *PBS NewsHour*, March 9, 2018, https://www.pbs.org/newshour/show/how-wrinkle-in-time-director-ava-duvernay-is-breaking-down-walls-in-hollywood.

This was something that Oprah Winfery: Ryzik, "Ava DuVernay's Fiercely Feminine."

"I grew up in an era": Ryzik, "Ava DuVernay's Fiercely Feminine."

It helped her realize: Ryzik, "Ava DuVernay's Fiercely Feminine."

"Civil rights work": Ryzik, "Ava DuVernay's Fiercely Feminine."

"An artist and an activist": Emma Goldberg, "Ava Duvernay's Fight for Change, Onscreen and Off," *New York Times*, July 8, 2020, https://www.nytimes.com/2020/07/08/movies/director-ava-duvernay-movies-police-protests.html.

"Living in it you don't": DuVernay, "Ava DuVernay Can't Stop."

at the time of the attack were: Aisha Harris, "The Central Park Five: 'We Were Just Baby Boys,'" *New York Times*, May 30, 2019, https://www.nytimes.com/2019/05/30/arts/television/when-they-see-us.html.

on the night in question: Deanna Paul, "'When They See Us' Tells the Important Story About the Central Park Five. Here's What It Leaves Out," *Washington Post*, June 29, 2019, https://www.washingtonpost .com/history/2019/06/29/when-they-see-us-tells-important-story -central-park-five-heres-what-it-leaves-out/.

In April 1861: "The Civil War and Emancipation," Africans in America, PBS, accessed July 1, 2021, https://www.pbs.org/wgbh/aia/part4 /4p2967.html.

"For this reason, the government": "Civil War and Emancipation," PBS.

"two different kinds": Ava DuVernay, "Documentary '13th' Argues Mass Incarceration Is an Extension of Slavery," interview by Michael Martin, Dec. 17, 2016, NPR, transcript and audio, 5:00, https://www .npr.org/2016/12/17/505996792/documentary-13th-argues-mass -incarceration-is-an-extension-of-slavery.

"the US accounts for 5%": Patrick Ryan, "Ava DuVernay: 13th Explores Mass Incarceration, 'Black Trauma,'" *USA Today*, September 30, 2016, https://www.usatoday.com/story/life/movies/2016/09/30/ava -duvernay-13th-new-york-film-festival-nyff-premiere/91289924/.

"Black trauma is not": Ryan, "13th Explores Mass Incarceration."

"If a star has to be coddled": DuVernay, "Ava DuVernay Can't Stop."

5. Regina King

"My mom told NBC": Mia McNiece, "Regina King on Being a Child Star on *227* and How She Stayed Grounded: 'It's Not an Easy Thing,'" *People*, September 16, 2020, https://people.com/movies/regina-king -opens-up-about-being-a-child-star-on-227-and-how-she-stayed -grounded/.

"Acting was a hobby": Danielle Henderson, "The Scene-Stealer," *Vulture*, accessed November 15, 2021, https://www.vulture.com/2015/12 /regina-king-hollywood-scene-stealer.html.

"It needed to happen": Henderson, "Scene-Stealer."

"I saw that a lot of us": Henderson, "Scene-Stealer."

"The good news for me": Regina King, "For Actress Regina King, a Childhood Gig Launched a Career in Hollywood," interview by Terry Gross, *Fresh Air*, NPR, March 21, 2016, transcript and audio, 21:12,

https://www.nhpr.org/national/2016-03-21/for-actress-regina-king-a
-childhood-gig-launched-a-career-in-hollywood.

"I'm not missing out": Henderson, "Scene-Stealer."

she agreed to be in: Debra Birnbaum, "Regina King Talks Embarking on
Her Second Career: Directing," *Variety*, March 2, 2016, https://variety
.com/2016/tv/features/regina-king-branches-out-into-directing
-1201718885/.

Before Regina turned it: Faith Karimi, "The Truth Behind the Famous
Meeting of Four Black Heroes in 'One Night in Miami,'" CNN, April
25, 2021, https://www.cnn.com/2021/04/25/entertainment/one-night
-in-miami-movie-trnd/index.html.

"I also thought Kemp's words": Salamishah Tillet, "Regina King: Speaking
Truth to Power Through Her Art," *New York Times*, January 15, 2021,
https://www.nytimes.com/2021/01/15/movies/regina-king-one-night
-in-miami.html.

"This subject has been": Tillet, "Speaking Truth to Power."

"He said it would help people": Birnbaum, "Her Second Career."

"It's tough, because you don't": Birnbaum, "Her Second Career."

6. Shoda Rhimes

"Don't you have enough?": Lacey Rose, "Shonda Rhimes Is Ready to
'Own Her S***': The Game-Changing Showrunner on Leaving ABC,
'Culture Shock' at Netflix and Overcoming Her Fears," *Hollywood
Reporter*, October 21, 2020, https://www.hollywoodreporter.com
/movies/movie-features/shonda-rhimes-is-ready-to-own-her-s-the
-game-changing-showrunner-on-leaving-abc-culture-shock-at
-netflix-and-overcoming-her-fears-4079375/.

Her creative brain is global: Shonda Rhimes, "My Year of Saying Yes to
Everything," TED, YouTube video, 18:44, uploaded March 9, 2016,
https://www.youtube.com/watch?v=gmj-azFbpkA.

During her time at ABC: Rhimes, "My Year of Saying Yes."

"I make up stuff": Shonda Rhimes, *Year of Yes: How to Dance It Out, Stand
in the Sun and Be Your Own Person* (New York: Simon and Schuster,
2016), 9.

"Imagining is now my job.": Rhimes, *Year of Yes*, 12–13.

"You never say yes": Rhimes, *Year of Yes*, 25.

but only after much hesitation: Rhimes, *Year of Yes*, 119.

"Wanna play?": Rhimes, *Year of Yes*, 153.

She started to wonder: Rhimes, "My Year of Saying Yes."

She wanted "to be in a place": Rose, "Showrunner on Leaving ABC."

Shonda still found herself: Rose, "Showrunner on Leaving ABC."

"I felt like I was dying": Rose, "Showrunner on Leaving ABC."

"It wasn't like I had": John Koblin, "Shonda Rhimes Describes Her Grand Netflix Ambitions," *New York Times*, July 20, 2018, https://www .nytimes.com/2018/07/20/business/media/shonda-rhimes-netflix -series.html.

"I knew exactly": Koblin, "Netflix Ambitions."

"The way I understand": Julia Quinn, "'Bridgerton' Author Julia Quinn on Working with Shonda Rhimes, Diversity, and Steamy Sex Scenes," interview by Tamron Hall, *Tamron Hall Show*, uploaded on January 25, 2021, YouTube video, 4:25, https://www.youtube.com/watch?v =Jb5aXPlR8WM.

"When you're the": Maureen Lee Lenker, "Kerry Washington Explains Why Shonda Rhimes Dislikes the Word 'Diversity,'" *Entertainment Weekly*, November 19, 2017, https://ew.com/tv/2017/11/19/shonda-rhimes -dislikes-word-diversity/.

"I don't know how you": Madeline Berg, "Shonda Rhimes Does Things the Shondaland Way, Thanks to Groundbreaking Netflix Deal," *Forbes*, June 2, 2021, https://www.forbes.com/sites/maddieberg/2021/06/02 /shonda-rhimes-does-things-the-shondaland-way-thanks-to -groundbreaking-netflix-deal-bridgerton/.

"I really appreciate learning": Taryn Finley, "Mara Brock Akil Broke the Mold for Black Characters on TV—and She Isn't Done Yet," *HuffPost*, February 5, 2021, https://www.huffpost.com/entry/maya-brock-akil -tv-creator-black-history-month_n_601c644cc5b66c385ef7e5ac.

"I naturally give": Finley, "Brock Akil Broke the Mold."

"And what it does is it keeps": Finley, "Brock Akil Broke the Mold."

7. Gina Prince-Bythewood

"She kept talking": Marc Cabrera, "Buzzing About 'Bees': Pacific Grove

Native Turned Film Director Gina Prince-Bythewood Ushers New Project to Big Screen," *Monterey Herald*, October 17, 2008, https://www.montereyherald.com/2008/10/17/buzzing-about-bees-pacific-grove-native-turned-film-director-gina-prince-bythewood-ushers-new-project-to-big-screen.

"There were no girls' leagues": Lindsey Bahr, "Hollywood Catches Up to Director Gina Prince-Bythewood," Associated Press, July 7, 2020, https://apnews.com/article/entertainment-us-news-kiki-layne-charlize-theron-movies-82f21ff9660b29b8a32382f9e16a1810.

"It's so much about ambition": Bahr, "Hollywood Catches Up."

"I wanted to see myself": Antonio Ferme, "Gina Prince-Bythewood Says 'When Harry Met Sally' Inspired Her to Make 'Love & Basketball,'" *Variety*, June 21, 2021, https://variety.com/2021/film/news/gina-prince-bythewood-when-harry-met-sally-inspired-love-and-basketball-1235001036/.

"This was a very personal": Ferme, "'When Harry Met Sally' Inspired."

"I remember one specific": Brian Davids, "'Love & Basketball' at 20: Gina Prince-Bythewood on Wanting to Make a Black 'When Harry Met Sally,'" *Hollywood Reporter*, April 21, 2020, https://www.hollywoodreporter.com/movies/movie-news/love-basketball-gina-prince-bythewood-wanting-make-a-black-harry-met-sally-1291248/.

"You still felt that": Gene Seymour, "Black Directors Look Beyond Their Niche," *New York Times*, January 9, 2009, https://www.nytimes.com/2009/01/11/movies/11seym.html?pagewanted=all.

"That was painful": Margy Rochlin, "The Bee Season," *DGA Quarterly*, Fall 2008, http://www.dga.org/Craft/DGAQ/All-Articles/0803-Fall-2008/Independent-Voice-Gina-Prince-Bythewood.aspx (brackets in original).

"Wait, I should be doing": Rochlin, "Bee Season."

"God, I've blown it.": Rochlin, "Bee Season."

"I wanted to find": Gina Prince-Bythewood, "Filmmaker Interview: Gina Prince-Bythewood," *Film Independent*, May 20, 2007, https://web.archive.org/web/20141129062350if_/http://www.filmindependent.org/news-and-blog/filmmaker-interview-gina-prince-bythewood/.

"*It really messed with my head*": Prince-Bythewood, "Filmmaker Interview."

"*That was how I felt*": Prince-Bythewood, "Filmmaker Interview."

"*And suddenly I just saw*": Gina Prince-Bythewood, "Exclusive: Gina Prince-Bythewood Talks Writing & Directing 'Beyond the Lights,'" interview by Shaina411, *Source*, November 14, 2014, https://thesource .com/2014/11/14/exclusive-gina-prince-bythewood-talks-writing -directing-beyond-the-lights/.

"*I love directing*": Prince-Bythewood, "'Beyond the Lights.'"

"*It was a love story*": Prince-Bythewood, "'Beyond the Lights.'"

"*One was the suicide*": NPR Staff, "Director Gina Prince-Bythewood: It's Time to 'Obliterate the Term Black Film,'" *Code Switch*, NPR, November 14, 2014, transcript and audio, 6:00, https://www.npr.org /sections/codeswitch/2014/11/14/363793023/director-gina-prince -bythewood-its-time-to-obliterate-the-term-black-film.

Gina "*saw the film*": Bilge Ebiri, "Director Gina Prince-Bythewood on *Beyond the Lights*, Creating Great Chemistry, and Shooting Love Scenes," *Vulture*, November 16, 2014, https://www.vulture.com/2014 /11/gina-prince-bythewood-interview-beyond-the-lights.html.

"*Everyone loved the script*": Ebiri, "*Beyond the Lights*."

"*I only do films*": Gina Prince-Bythewood, "Black Women's Stories Are the Hardest to Get Made: The Gina Prince-Bythewood Interview," interview by Tambay Obenson, *Indiewire*, April 22, 2020, https://www .indiewire.com/2020/04/gina-prince-bythewood-interview-love-and -basketball-1202223823/.

8. Kimberly Peirce

"*I was completely obsessed*": Kimberly Peirce, "As 'Boys Don't Cry' Joins National Film Registry, Kimberly Peirce Addresses Its Complicated History," interview by Jude Dry, *Indiewire*, December 12, 2019, https://www.indiewire.com/2019/12/kimberly-peirce-interview-boys -dont-cry-transgender-1202196536/.

It raised public awareness: Katrina Markel, "The Legacy of the 'Boys Don't Cry' Hate Crime 20 Years Later," Buzzfeed, January 9, 2014, https:// www.buzzfeed.com/katrinamarkel/the-legacy-of-the-boys-dont-cry -hate-crime-20-years-later.

Notes

"sometimes, teachers tell": Jack Wang, "Kimberly Peirce Reflects on
How UChicago Shaped Her Filmmaking Career," *UChicago News*,
November 19, 2019, https://news.uchicago.edu/story/kimberly-peirce
-how-uchicago-shaped-her-career.

"I didn't really have": Kimberly Peirce, "In Conversation: Kimberly Peirce
on 'Boys Don't Cry,' Twenty Years Later," interview by Anya Jaremko-
Greenwold, *Flood*, October 7, 2019, https://floodmagazine.com/69107
/in-conversation-kimberly-peirce-on-boys-dont-cry-twenty-years
-later/.

"moves to live": Kimberly Peirce, "Trans Translated: *Boys Don't Cry*
Director Kimberly Peirce on 20 Years of Queer Culture," interview by
Stephanie Fairyington, *Elle*, February 7, 2014, https://www.elle.com
/culture/career-politics/interviews/a12663/kimberly-peirce-interview/.

"Gender identity can": Peirce, "Trans Translated."

a "stunning debut": Janet Maslin, "Film Festival Reviews; Sometimes
Accepting an Identity Means Accepting a Fate, Too," *New York Times*,
October 1, 1999.

"one of the best films": Roger Ebert, "Boys Don't Cry," RogerEbert.com,
October 22, 1999, https://www.rogerebert.com/reviews/boys-dont
-cry-1999.

"although Hilary Swank": Ebert, "Boys Don't Cry."

"She captured": Jessica Fargen, "Fox Settles Lawsuit with Woman Depicted
in 'Boys Don't Cry,'" *Yankton Daily Press & Dakotan*, March 22, 2000,
https://www.yankton.net/news/article_182a829c-fe47-5047-ba81
-e089102b2880.html.

"to find somebody": Peirce, "'Boys Don't Cry' Joins National Film Registry."

"Given that I'm": Peirce, "As 'Boys Don't Cry' Joins National Film Registry."

Though surprised at the vehemence: Scott Jaschik, "Who's Intolerant?,"
Inside Higher Ed, December 12, 2016, https://www.insidehighered
.com/news/2016/12/12/reed-college-engages-soul-searching-after
-posters-and-shouts-insult-director-boys.

"You are the power": Peirce, "Peirce on 'Boys Don't Cry'" (ellipsis and
brackets in original).

The "interferences against": Peirce, "Peirce on 'Boys Don't Cry.'"

"Why are the women": Peirce, "Peirce on 'Boys Don't Cry.'"

9. Dee Rees

she had to pick up trash: Jenna Wortham, "Dee Rees and the Art of Surviving as a Black Female Director," *New York Times Magazine*, February 6, 2020, https://www.nytimes.com/2020/02/06/magazine/dee-rees-black-female-director.html.

"[The theater owners] weren't selling out": Rebecca Keegan, "Director Dee Rees on the Importance of Debut 'Pariah' Becoming a Criterion Release: 'We Have to Widen the Canon,'" *Hollywood Reporter*, June 17, 2021, https://www.hollywoodreporter.com/movies/movie-features/dee-rees-pariah-criteron-release-1234967676/ (brackets in original).

"It shaped me" : Keegan, "'Pariah' Becoming Criterion Release."

"They were positioning": Keegan, "'Pariah' Becoming Criterion Release."

"My parents thought": Wortham, "Rees and the Art of Surviving."

"I failed and I failed hard": Wortham, "Rees and the Art of Surviving."

"This double-whammy": David Canfield, "Dee Rees Talks Queer Filmmaking, Recent Setbacks, and Waiting to Do It All," *Entertainment Weekly*, May 22, 2020, https://ew.com/movies/dee-rees-talks-queer-filmmaking/.

"I'm just interested in seeing": Aramide Tinubu, "'Pariah' at 10: Dee Rees' Groundbreaking Debut Paved the Way for 'Moonlight' and 'Pose,'" *Indiewire*, May 7, 2021, https://www.indiewire.com/2021/05/pariah-dee-rees-moonlight-pose-1234635645/.

"include restored film transfers": Criterion Collection, "FAQ," accessed July 5, 2021, https://www.criterion.com/faq.

In 2020 the New York Times *reported*: Kyle Buchanan and Reggie Ugwu, "How the Criterion Collection Crops Out African-American Directors," *New York Times*, Aug. 20, 2020, https://www.nytimes.com/interactive/2020/08/20/movies/criterion-collection-african-americans.html.

"We hope that the breadth": Keegan, "'Pariah' Becoming Criterion Release."

"It was about convincing": Canfield, "Rees Talks Queer Filmmaking."

10. Chloé Zhao

"I try to capture": Samuel Harries, "Italian Neorealism," Movements in Film, https://www.movementsinfilm.com/italian-neorealism.

Notes

"an ancient culture": John Powers, "How Chloé Zhao Reinvented the Western," *Vogue*, March 22, 2018, https://www.vogue.com/article /chloe-zhao-the-rider-vogue-april-2018.

"The script, the story": Scott Macaulay, "Chloé Zhao: 25 New Faces of Independent Film," *Filmmaker*, August 14, 2013, https://web.archive .org/web/20201030224312/https://filmmakermagazine.com/people /chloe-zhao/ (brackets in original).

"It goes back": Macaulay, "25 New Faces."

"Since its initial": Suyin Haynes, "Here's Why Chloé Zhao's Oscars Win Was Censored in China," *Time*, April 27, 2021, https://time.com /5959003/chloe-zhao-oscars-censorship/.

"what drives Zhao's film": Powers, "Zhao Reinvented the Western."

"listen well": Chloé Zhao, Joshua James Richards, and Mollye Asher, "First Films with Chloé Zhao: Nomadland," interview by Ryan Silbert, Metrograph Live Screenings, March 3, 2021.

"practical locations": Kate Aurthur, "Chloé Zhao on Making Oscars History and How She Stayed True to Herself Directing Marvel's 'Eternals,'" *Variety*, April 28, 2021, https://variety.com/2021/film /directors/chloe-zhao-oscars-nomadland-marvel-eternals-dracula -1234961719/.

"The TV projects": Cara Buckley, "The Woman Behind 'Wonder Woman,'" *New York Times*, June 1, 2017, https://www.nytimes.com/2017/06/01 /movies/wonder-woman-gal-gadot-patty-jenkins.html.

11. Petra Costa

"a book of life": Petra Costa, "Elena: Entrevista com a Directora Petra Costa," interview by Juliana Varella, *Guia da Semana*, May 8, 2013, https://www.guiadasemana.com.br/cinema/noticia/elena-entrevista -com-a-diretora-petra-costa (my translation).

"The moment I arrived": "A Family Tragedy: Finding Solace Through Film," *Barnard Magazine*, Summer 2013, https://barnard.edu/magazine /summer-2013/family-tragedy.

"a balance of": Costa, "Elena."

"It was a mixture of": Petra Costa, "Entrevista Exclusiva—Petra Costa Fala Sobre o Documentário Elena," interview by Francisco Russo,

AdoroCinema, May 9, 2013, https://www.adorocinema.com/noticias
/filmes/noticia-102960/(my translation).

"really challenging the system": "Why Director Sarah Polley Is a National
Treasure," CBC, July 6, 2020, https://www.cbc.ca/television/why
-director-sarah-polley-is-a-national-treasure-1.5632852.

"was my birthright": Petra Costa, "'The Edge of Democracy' with Director
Petra Costa," interview by Michael Brooks, *The Michael Brooks Show*,
YouTube video, 6:32, uploaded February 4, 2020, https://www
.youtube.com/watch?v=op-DAwcJ_SE.

"It became a trauma": "'Edge of Democracy,' Q and A with Director Petra
Costa, MoMA Film," Museum of Modern Art, YouTube video, 25:20,
uploaded February 4, 2020, https://www.youtube.com/watch?v
=ZPghRC3G-60.

"searing and enlightening": A. O. Scott, "Review: 'Edge of Democracy'
Looks at Brazil with Outrage and Heartbreak," *New York Times*, June
18, 2019, https://www.nytimes.com/2019/06/18/movies/edge-of
-democracy-review.html.

12. Mindy Kaling

At this time, Mindy is both: Devon Ivie, "The Rise and Rise of Mindy
Kaling," *Vulture*, February 26, 2019, https://www.vulture.om/2018/03
/mindy-kaling-evolution.html.

"bonded over comedy": Mindy Kaling, *Is Everyone Hanging Out Without
Me? (And Other Concerns)* (New York: Three Rivers Press, 2011)
35–36.

"I was freakin' jaws": Kaling, *Is Everyone Hanging Out*, 47.

she *"was famously one of the worst"*: Kaling, *Is Everyone Hanging Out*, 50.

"I spent hours sitting": Kaling, *Is Everyone Hanging Out*, 55.

"Because no one was hiring": Kaling, *Is Everyone Hanging Out*, 85.

"We did no research": Kaling, *Is Everyone Hanging Out*, 87.

"We'd hear the door": Kaling, *Is Everyone Hanging Out*, 94.

"Joking around with Brenda": Kaling, *Is Everyone Hanging Out*, 111.

"Most of the time": Kaling, *Is Everyone Hanging Out*, 107.

"This was the smallest amount": Kaling, *Is Everyone Hanging Out*, 110.

the *"sitcom equivalent"*: Ken Tucker, "'The Mindy Project' Went Out Exactly the Way Mindy Wanted It To," *Huffington Post*, November 14, 2017, https://www.huffpost.com/entry/the-mindy-project-went-out-exactly -the-way-mindy-kaling-wanted-it-to_n_5a0b525de4b00a6eece4ddc0.

"I [didn't] want to wake up": Kaitlin Reilly and Stacy Jackman, "Mindy Kaling on Single Parenting and Why 'The Biggest Reward Is Seeing How Happy My Children Are," *Yahoo Life*, January 24, 2022, https:// www.yahoo.com/lifestyle/mindy-kaling-interview-single-mother -pandemic-parenting-160608164.html (brackets in original).

13. Lulu Wang

"tears of joy": Lulu Wang, "What You Don't Know," *This American Life*, episode 585, "In Defense of Ignorance," April 22, 2016, audio, 58:55, https://www.thisamericanlife.org/585/in-defense-of-ignorance/act -one-7.

"That's China": Wang, "What You Don't Know."

Despite knowing multiple languages: Lulu Wang, "Filmmaker Lulu Wang Based 'The Farewell' on Her Family's Real-Life Lie," interview by Terry Gross, *Fresh Air*, NPR, July 24, 2019, transcript and audio, 36:00, https://www.npr.org/2019/07/24/744805282/filmmaker-lulu -wang-based-the-farewell-on-her-family-s-real-life-lie.

"Posthumous still manages": Sarah Kurchak, "Film Review: Posthumous," *Consequence*, July 8, 2015, https://consequence.net/2015/07/film -review-posthumous/.

"When I was first pitching": Jake Coyle, "In 'The Farewell,' a Family Drama Straddling East and West," Associated Press, July 10, 2019, https:// apnews.com/article/d8586aee05494be898da5d3347ea7393.

"how wonderfully raw": David Fear, "'The Farewell': Lulu Wang's Truth, Lies, and the Long Goodbye," *Rolling Stone*, July 16, 2019, https:// www.rollingstone.com/movies/movie-features/the-farewell-lulu-wang -interview-854868/.

"about the family": Fear, "'The Farewell.'"

"the most exciting": Eric Kohn, "'The Farewell': Lulu Wang Made the Year's Most Exciting Hit by Refusing to Whitewash It," *Indiewire*, July 18, 2019, https://www.indiewire.com/2019/07/the-farewell-lulu-wang -interview-a24-1202158932/.

"Sidestepping the temptations": Justin Chang, "Review: Lulu Wang's Delightful 'The Farewell,' Starring Awkwafina, Shows Us a Family Divided," *Los Angeles Times*, July 9, 2019, https://www.latimes.com /entertainment/movies/la-et-mn-the-farewell-review-awkwafina -20190709-story.html.

"[Nai Nai's] friend saw": Matthew Dessem, "Lulu Wang's Grandmother Learned That She Has Cancer from *The Farewell*, Lulu Wang's Film About Not Telling Her Grandmother She Has Cancer," *Slate*, January 5, 2020, https://slate.com/culture/2020/01/farewell-lulu-wang -grandmother-learns-secret-hollywood-foreign-press-foreign -language-symposium.html.

"I got to share": Fear "'The Farewell.'"

14. Greta Gerwig

"I recently went back": Greta Gerwig, "Greta Gerwig on Lena Dunham, Yale (NSFW) and Scott Rudin," interview by Catie Lazarus, *Employee of the Month*, produced by Slate Podcasts, podcast, March 9, 2016, https://www.podchaser.com/podcasts/employee-of-the-month-4886 /episodes/greta-gerwig-on-lena-dunham-ya-236325.

"I was more": "Lady Bird Interview, Director Greta Gerwig," interview by Dana Han-Klein, The DHK, YouTube video, 12:07, uploaded November 10, 2017, https://www.youtube.com/watch?v =nP2ymKPq45c.

"a rare and wonderful": Sarah Mink, "'Frances Ha' Is a Rare and Wonderful Film About Mess and Friendship," Bitch Media, June 7, 2013, https:// www.bitchmedia.org/post/frances-ha-is-a-rare-and-wonderful-film -about-mess-and-friendship.

"It's not for us": Greta Gerwig and Saoirse Ronan, "Greta Gerwig and Saoirse Ronan on the Importance of Female Voices in Hollywood, Times Talks," interview by Frank Bruni, New York Times Events, YouTube video, 1:03:45, uploaded January 5, 2018, https://www .youtube.com/watch?v=M4eS4-O8ptw.

"if [they] were raised": Christine Smallwood, "Greta Gerwig's Radical Confidence," *New York Times Magazine*, November 1, 2017, https://

www.nytimes.com/2017/11/01/magazine/greta-gerwigs-radical
-confidence.html?searchResultPosition=1.

"Nothing, then a lot": Gerwig and Ronan, "Importance of Female Voices in
Hollywood."

"[Mia] said that": Smallwood, "Greta Gerwig's Radical Confidence."

In other words, each talented: Gerwig and Ronan, "Importance of Female
Voices in Hollywood."

15. Issa Rae

"Growing up as a young": Issa Rae, "Black Folk Don't Like to Be Told
They're Not Black," *HuffPost*, August 4, 2011, https://www.huffpost
.com/entry/black-folk-dont-movie_b_912660.

"I remember being excited": DeNeen L. Brown, "Issa Rae and Her Web
Series 'The Misadventures of Awkward Black Girl' Are Rising Stars,"
Washington Post, October 4, 2012, https://www.washingtonpost.com
/lifestyle/magazine/issa-rae-and-her-web-series-the-misadventures-of
-awkward-black-girl-are-rising-stars/2012/10/01/bf3c04a4-fc2b-11e1
-8adc-499661afe377_story.html.

"Who I was was not acceptable": Brown, "Rae and Her Web Series."

She recalled in a personal essay: Rae, "Black Folk."

she "realized there was more": Rae, "Black Folk."

"A Different World made me": Issa Rae, *The Misadventures of Awkward
Black Girl*, (New York: 37 Ink/Atria, 2015), 40.

Issa found "a sort of solace": Rae, *Awkward Black Girl*, 40.

"I was in the hub": Rae, *Awkward Black Girl*, 40.

"Every year for four years": Rae, *Awkward Black Girl*, 41.

"Looking back, I had no idea": Rae, *Awkward Black Girl*, 44.

"How hard is it to portray": Rae, *Awkward Black Girl*, 44.

"it came to me I was awkward": Brown, "Rae and Her Web Series."

"I would have been indefinitely": Rae, *Awkward Black Girl*, 46.

"If it weren't for social media": Rae, *Awkward Black Girl*, 46.

"The universal gender classification": Rae, *Awkward Black Girl*, 46.

"A phone conversation": Jenna Wortham, "The Misadventures of Issa Rae,"
New York Times Magazine, August 4, 2015, https://www.nytimes.com
/2015/08/09/magazine/the-misadventures-of-issa-rae.html.

"It's more complicated": Rae, *Awkward Black Girl*, 46.

"I compromised my vision": Wortham, "The Misadventures."

"I remember being on the set": Issa Rae, "Issa Rae Embraces Her Role as a Hollywood Trailblazer: 'You Can't Be Polite or Modest,'" interview by Jessica Herndon, *Hollywood Reporter*, August 19, 2020, https://www.hollywoodreporter.com/movies/movie-features/issa-rae-embraces-her-role-as-a-hollywood-trailblazer-you-cant-be-polite-or-modest-4047809.

"It was just like, 'I'm going'": Herndon, "Hollywood Trailblazer."

"I'm definitely interested in class": Jonah Weiner, "Why 'Candyman' and 'Captain Marvel 2' Director Nia DaCosta Will Make History in 2021," *Wall Street Journal*, January 13, 2021, https://www.wsj.com/articles/nia-dacosta-marvel-captain-america-2-director-candyman-11610544651

As a Black woman growing up: Weiner, "DaCosta Will Make History" (brackets in original).

"The lack of imagination": Jenelle Riley, "10 Directors to Watch: Nia DaCosta Remakes 'Candyman' for Jordan Peele," *Variety*, February 25, 2021, https://variety.com/2021/film/features/10-directors-to-watch-nia-dacosta-candyman-1234914974/.